A Tale of
Two Owners

A Tale of Two Owners

Achieving Exit Success
Between Business Co-Owners

Patrick A. Ungashick

_BOOK_LOGIX®
Alpharetta, GA

ISBN: 978-1-61005-808-7
Library of Congress Control Number: 2016913975

10 9 8 7 6 5 4 3 2   1 0 2 5 1 6

Printed in the United States of America

∞This paper meets the requirements of ANSI/NISO Z39.48-1992 (Permanence of Paper)

For Maggie, who inspires me.

If we are together, nothing is impossible.
If we are divided, all will fail.
　　　　　　　　—Winston Churchill

If you like a person, you say, "Let's go into
business together." Man is a social animal after
all, but such partnerships are fraught with danger.
　　　　　　　　—Brian Tracy

Contents

Author's Note

This book discusses various tax, legal, and financial matters associated with developing and implementing a successful exit plan. While the author has made the best effort to carefully and accurately present these matters, each business owner must take into account his or her specific situation and consult with his or her advisors before reaching any conclusions or taking action. The reader would grow tedious if every point ended with "Please consult your tax, legal, and financial advisors on your specific situation." However, that is exactly what is required.

Introduction

The image of the business owner alone at the top is a myth. About 70 percent of the six million privately held businesses in the United States have more than one owner, and the average number of owners per business is nearly three.[*] This means there are approximately twelve million US business co-owners. Practically all of them want to successfully exit from their businesses one day, and practically all of them will find that their path to exiting successfully requires aligning their exit plans with those of their co-owners. This is where the challenge begins.

Put two or more business co-owners together, and it is virtually inevitable that they will have different exit goals. For example, one co-owner wants to exit sooner; another wants to exit later. One wants to sell the business; another wants to pass it down to his or her children. One needs more money at exit to be happy; another needs less. One wants a quick exit; another wants to stay with the company for longer. Sometimes the different exit goals are only partially or marginally conflicting. In many situations, however, the co-owners' different exit goals are incompatible, meaning the pursuit and fulfillment of one co-owner's goals will undermine or block another co-owner from achieving his goals.

Exit-goal incompatibility is the natural byproduct of the inescapable human differences among co-owners. Some co-owners are younger, some older. Some have smaller families; some have bigger families. Some spend less

---

[*] CMI. *Business Owners Exit Readiness Market Research Survey*. 2009. White Horse Advisors, Atlanta.

money; some spend more. These differences often present no issues during the years the co-owners are working side by side with the common goal of growing their business. At exit, however, the co-owners may find themselves pulling in opposite directions, unsure of how this predicament came to be and clueless as to what to do about it.

The purpose of this book is to help co-owners achieve successful exits to benefit not only themselves, but also each other, their families, their business, and their employees and customers. Helping co-owners achieve successful exits may be the most important and least addressed issue affecting baby-boomer business owners. In my more than twenty-five years working with owners of small to medium, privately held companies, I have witnessed countless co-owners struggle to under-stand why their goals at exit are in conflict. If left unaddressed, goal incompatibility at a minimum causes stress, strained relationships, stunted business growth, increased risk, and more expensive and difficult exits. At its worst, exit-goal incompatibility can lead to broken relationships, millions in lost business value, legal confrontations, and outright failed exits.

Business co-owners commonly face some degree of goal incompatibility at exit, yet the issue is not widely recognized. Many co-owners do not discuss exit as a topic until late in their career, and thus are unaware that they have incompatible goals. Once co-owners finally realize that they face goal incompatibility, co-owners often put off dealing with these issues for fear of damaging their relationship with one another. Also, this is not a topic co-owners readily admit to outsiders. Few co-owners would want their customers, employees, competitors, or peers to know these internal challenges are occurring. Finally, exit often seems far enough in the future, and the company has enough immediate needs, that co-owners often (wrongly) conclude that dealing with their exit incompatibilities can wait for another day without causing harm.

Business owners and co-owners often wait too long to develop their exit plans. Stephen Covey, author of *The 7 Habits of Highly Effective People*, shared that those who "begin with the end in mind" are typically more successful than those who do not. Likewise, co-owners should also keep their exit strategies in mind, even from the beginning. There are two primary reasons to start working now on your exit plans. First, there is no way to know if the decisions you make today will lead to exit success or shortfall if you do not have clearly defined exit goals. As this book attempts to show, many business decisions made in the present time seem to be sound and proper, but when exit draws near, those decisions hinder or undermine successful exits.

Second, many of the legal, tax, financial, and other tactics and tools to help co-owners exit successfully take years to implement and reach full effectiveness. The less lead time co-owners allot themselves to prepare for exit, the harder things become because they have fewer options and less flexibility. If you or your co-owners have five years or less remaining until a desired exit, you have reached crunch time.

This book tells the story of Al Beaman and Robert Gilmore, co-owners of Ark Technology Solutions Inc. After seventeen years side by side building a business together, they come to realize that their exit goals are incompatible and lack an easy solution. It's a fable that deals with a critical issue—how can one owner happily exit when achieving his goals means denying a successful exit to the other? While Al and Robert are characters of fiction, their story is all too common. It is my hope that through their story, you will gain an understanding of what you and your co-owners may face and how to address it. As author and speaker Brené Brown said in her popular TED Talk entitled "The Power of Vulnerability," "Stories are just data with a soul."

Following "The Fable," you will find "The Guide to Creating Co-Owner Exit Alignment." The Guide explores the challenges business co-owners face at exit, explains why exit-goal incompatibility occurs, and lays out a step-by-step course of action for co-owners to achieve alignment. Note that alignment does not mean matching or identical goals. Co-owners can and usually will have different exit goals and plans. Alignment means the co-owners' individual goals are calibrated to be in sync, such that one co-owner's goals will not interfere with or undermine another co-owner's exit success. The book is structured so that should the reader need quick answers and help, you may skip directly to the Guide. For most readers, however, let the Guide be your reference material to consult after you have taken the journey with Al and Robert.

Exit is inevitable. Even if you prefer to work until your health or life is exhausted, every business owner must address how his or her exit impacts family, co-owners, employees, customers, and the business itself. Your future deserves your present attention; if you are like most business owners, you have worked too hard and accomplished too much to surrender control over the eventual outcome. **Every business owner needs an exit plan**.

Yet business co-owners have to go one step further. They must consider and create exit plans that provide for not only their success, but also enable others to enjoy exit success too. Planning ahead not only gives you the opportunity to one day dance in the end zone, it also creates the chance for your co-owners to share the dance with you.

The Fable

Week 1

Monday, about 5:00 p.m.,
at the offices of Ark Technology Solutions Inc.

Al sat at his desk, absently turning over in his hands a small wooden ark, wondering what had gone wrong. His daughters had given him the model ship on the first Father's Day after starting up this company. That had been seventeen years ago. Al usually felt that the last seventeen years of co-owning and leading this business with his partner Robert were the best years of his career. On days like today, however, he wondered if their relationship's good years were mostly behind them.

It was not uncommon for Robert to disagree with Al on a business issue. Al knew that one of the reasons the two of them had worked well together for as long as they had was because they were different people with different points of view. Their differences more often than not complemented one another and made their company stronger. Recently, however, the different points of view seemed to be growing—so much so that Al sensed he and Robert were no longer on the same page. Worse, for reasons Al could not pin down, it seemed that they were not trying as hard as they once did to make business decisions together.

A smile crossed Al's face as he remembered how they used to make important business decisions when they first started Ark Technology Solutions. Their company was founded in the den of Al's 1950s brick ranch in Marietta, Georgia, an architectural style that Robert teasingly referred to as "brick double-wide." Back then, the business co-owners developed a routine for making important business decisions. They would meet in the den and lock the door, not leaving until the matter at hand was resolved. Their self-imposed confinement was more symbolic than substance. They could unlock the door and let themselves out at any time, and the old door's handle was so loose that it popped open whenever the house's air-conditioning system kicked on (which during Georgia summers meant all the time). Not to mention the fact that in the beginning they had no employees other than themselves, so it was unclear exactly who they were locking out of the room. That was a long time ago, so long that there were three owners of Ark Technology Solutions at the time. With a heavy frown, Al grew angry with himself for remembering that part of the story. He immediately refocused on the day's events, the fond memory pushed from his mind.

Reflecting on how they used to work together made Al feel even wearier than he already felt after the discussion earlier that day. Al could not understand why he and Robert seemed to be at odds more frequently as of late. Today was a perfect example. Al, Robert, and Dan Alvarez had been talking about a new salesperson Dan was potentially hiring to the sales team. During their conversation, Dan mentioned Al's idea about cutting the commission rates for their salespeople on project-related work. Robert immediately objected to this idea. Al could understand why Robert might have some concerns. After all, with Dan in the room, Al had not been able to explain to Robert all the reasons for making this change. What had surprised him was how strongly Robert protested against the idea, going so far as to become visibly agitated. That, to Al, made little sense. Sales was not part of Robert's responsibilities; he headed up operations.

Al needed to get with Robert, in private, and explain why he was going to make this change. Their company needed less project work and more new customers for its core business, ongoing IT support services. They had created Ark to provide small businesses with high quality, continuous technology service solutions. The project-related work that they increasingly found themselves doing brought in cash, but it consumed precious resources. Worse, most projects were done within a few weeks or months. Their company needed revenue streams that lasted years.

Al was used to his younger partner wearing his emotions on his sleeve. That's one reason why employees liked Robert—he was passionate, as well as honest and friendly. In turn, when Robert was bothered or upset, it was not difficult to know how he felt. Even so, Al could not fathom why Robert became so unusually worked up today.

Al's intention to think about this issue further, to figure out why he and his partner were not on the same page, was interrupted by the chirping of his phone. Al put the wooden ark down, slid on his reading glasses, and picked up his phone. The small LCD screen flashed, "You're on— 5:30!" The message lifted his mood. His retired neighbor Tom Higgins was accepting an offer to play a quick round of nine holes at their club before Al would be due home for dinner. Quickly grabbing his phone and briefcase, Al made for the door. There was time enough to figure out this issue with Robert, he told himself. Besides, business was booming. Customers were spending money. Profits were up. Employees were happy. It was a beautiful Southern spring day. At ten minutes past five p.m., Al made for his car in his reserved space in the employee parking lot, thinking that if he hurried he might be able to get in a few practice putts before teeing off.

***

Robert sat at his desk, worried that an hour would not be enough time to return all of the e-mails and calls he needed to get to and still get out the door by six p.m. to make his youngest son's soccer game. He had missed the last several games. His son never said anything, but missing games bothered Robert and he knew it bothered his son. It was one thing if Robert missed a game because he was traveling, but today he was not on the road, so he didn't have any excuses.

As Robert opened up his e-mail inbox, his eyes caught a picture hanging on the wall over his computer screen. In the picture, Al and Robert stood with two other people, the foursome posing for the ubiquitous golf pre-tee-off lineup photo. Robert clearly remembered that day. It was about five years ago at East Lake, one of Atlanta's finest golf courses. The two people in the photo accompanying them were John Goodson and Betsy Cunningham, executives from Asperon Inc., one of Ark's largest customers then and now. Seeing the picture triggered something in Robert, and he paused before proceeding with his e-mails.

He had spoken to Betsy just last week about a potential new expansion project for Asperon Inc., which could be a six-figure engagement for Ark this year. Why would Al want to reduce the commissions they paid to their salespeople now, when projects like this were out there? It made no sense to him. After being partners with Al for seventeen years, Robert felt like he knew the man pretty well. Al was never one to shy away from chasing down work for their company. If Robert remembered correctly, about five years ago Al helped sell to

Asperon one of the first big projects Ark had ever done. Asperon's newest project would likely generate higher profit margins than the traditional service side of their business. To Robert, cutting commissions to salespeople was the same as saying, "We don't want this type of business." Although it made no sense to Robert, Al's actions were not completely out of character as of late. Robert found himself getting surprised more and more frequently by his older partner. Still fixated on the picture, Robert realized that he could not remember the last time Al participated in a meeting with Asperon, or even spoke to them. The realization stood out for him. It was not that long ago that Al would never have missed an opportunity to be in the room with a large customer.

Now completely forgetting about pending e-mails and phone messages, Robert leaned back into his desk chair, bothered by this line of thinking. He felt, for the first time, that he and Al were not on the same page. Worse, Robert could see that he and his partner never "locked the door" anymore, as they used to do in Al's den to talk through tough issues and make decisions. Al's den—how long had it been since he had thought of that shabby old room? Picturing its chocolate-brown laminated walls, slightly less-brown carpeting, and creaking, maroon, vinyl furniture made him cringe. Those were the old days, but not necessarily the good days. They had K. to thank for that. All these years later and Al still preferred to not even think the other man's full name, much less say it.

Robert surprised himself. He had not thought about K. in a long time. Robert felt his face flush with anger. Fighting off a negative mood, he pushed the memory away. Their company had come a long way since then, mostly for the better. Robert wanted to focus on today, not the past. So how had he and Al gotten off course?

As Robert contemplated this, a repeating buzz in his pocket brought him back into the present. He pulled out his cell phone. Its screen indicated 5:10 p.m. Frustrated with himself, he let the incoming call go to voice mail. He had other calls to address first. He would figure out later what was wrong with Al. Besides, business was booming. Customers were spending money. Profits were up. Employees were happy. Robert needed to return at least some of these e-mails and calls before rushing out the door. He would not miss tonight's soccer game.

Approximately five years earlier in the main conference room at Ark Technology Solutions Inc.

"We really like the work Ark does to maintain Asperon's computer network, so we felt it was natural to come to you for our CRM project," John Goodson explained to Al and Robert. "We are eager to find a vendor who can help us, because we need this expansion. We have outgrown our existing CRM system. If we don't get this new system installed and our people trained, we are going to run into some serious problems."

Betsy Cunningham nodded in agreement. "Yes, but I do have a question. Does Ark do this type of work? I mean John is right—we are happy with your ongoing IT support services. Yet this project is different, and of a much bigger scope. Can your company handle it?"

Al and Robert turned to each other to see who would field Betsy's question. After twelve years working together, they could read each other well. Robert saw that Al wanted to respond. "Yes, we can do the work and do it well," Al said, a touch of pride shining through. "We know your needs and systems well," he continued, "and have a track record of good service to you. After all, that's what an ark symbolizes—protection and safety no matter how bad the storm."

Betsy nodded her head in recognition of Al's last point, but then replied, "Yes, we are pleased with Ark. However, this project is different from what you do for us already. It's imperative that we get this done right and on time. Do you have the staff and bandwidth to handle this project in the manner we talked about today?"

Robert saw it was his turn to reply. "Actually, John and Betsy, to handle this project we would need to add resources, including several new staff positions. But we are prepared to do that. We have several other customers talking to us about similar needs, so even though your CRM project would be done and finished in about six months, we believe we can use the new staff on other projects with different customers. So if you don't mind me saying, your growth is going to help us grow too."

John and Betsy both paused, absorbing the answers they heard. John spoke next. "Well, we trust you. If you say you can do it, that goes pretty far with us. We will need a proposal, of course. If the numbers look right, the project is yours."

John and Betsy rose from the conference table. Al and Robert took the cue, rose as well, and all four shook hands.

Monday, about 7:30 p.m., at the Beaman residence

Al's round of nine holes did not prove to be his finest outing, but it was great just to get out and play. One of the advantages of living in Atlanta was he could golf at least nine months out of the year, and he wanted to take full advantage of the early warm weather. Pulling into the garage, he knew his wife would be eager for him to clean up, change, and head back out for a sushi dinner. With their two kids long since grown and out of the house, Albert and Valerie Beaman enjoyed the life's freedom that an empty nest and disposable income brought them.

It had not always been that way. Al and Valerie spent years working hard to create a life for themselves and their family. Valerie was scheduled to retire in two years after almost three decades in teaching, most of which was spent instructing fourth-grade classrooms at the local public elementary school. Al worked hard all his life too, first with IBM and then several smaller technology companies before launching Ark. That had been a risky venture. There were times when only Valerie's teaching salary put food on their table. Yet it had paid off. Al now felt he deserved golf a few times per week, and Valerie deserved sushi whenever she wanted. Walking in from the garage, Al heard his wife of thirty-nine years on the telephone in another room. He used the opportunity to pour a glass of wine and duck down the back hallway toward their bedroom to quickly shower and change clothes.

Forty minutes later, the couple found themselves seated at the sushi counter at Tama, their favorite local Japanese restaurant. Only a few minutes from the house, the restaurant boasted excellent service and a world-class chef who had managed to make a name for himself in the trendy but crowded Atlanta restaurant scene. With an Asahi beer for Al and a chardonnay for Valerie, a plate of steamed edamame beans dusted with sea salt, and an appetizer of the chef's selection of sashimi and nigiri, the world seemed pretty good.

At first they spoke about each of their day's activities, yet it was not long before Al could tell his wife was holding something back. He had spent about two-thirds of his life with her, and he knew her well. "What's on your mind, love?" he asked, pausing between bites of sashimi so she would see he was fully listening.

"I'm so glad you asked!" his wife quickly replied. "I finally found the perfect home in Tuscany. It was fully booked, but they just had a cancellation for July. I have some pictures saved on my phone to show you. Oh, Al, it's beyond amazing. It's a miracle it is even available at this point. We really need to reserve it—tonight, I think. That is, assuming you like it, of course."

Al couldn't help but smile. His wife was always quick to point out to him when he was on the verge of making a decision for the two of them without consulting her, but when she did it, well, that was another thing. Almost four decades of marriage had taught him to let it go. "It sounds great, and yes, I'd like to see the pictures. Were you really thinking a full month, though? I know you are off for the summer, but that's a long time for me to be away from the business." The look on Valerie's face told him that either she ate a piece of bad sushi, or he had said the wrong thing. Guessing it was the latter, Al correctly anticipated what came next.

"Al, come on. We only have a fortieth anniversary once. Yes, we need to go for a month. This house and most of the others will not rent for less than thirty days. That's not really the main reason, though. We have earned this time together." Valerie paused, watching her husband while mixing more wasabi in her soy sauce.

"When, Al?" Valerie continued, breaking the awkward silence. "When are you going to retire? I am done after next year. If I am retired and you are still going to work every day, where does that leave us? That's not the life we want, is it? I know it's not what I want."

"Love, we have talked about this before. I don't want to retire—not fully, at least. Whatever I decide, I just can't see myself doing nothing all day even after my exit from the company."

"Retire—exit—whatever. You know what I am talking about, Al," Valerie said in frustration.

"Yes, I hear you. I want what you want. I assure you, love, that in three to five years I will exit from Ark."

Now Al could see his wife was upset, and it was not the food.

"Al," Valerie said, intentionally drawing out his name, "unlike you, I have been keeping track. Do you remember when we talked about this same issue last fall? We were at the lake, sitting on the porch by ourselves. The kids were out in the boat. Do you remember what you said to me then? You told me then you would be ready to exit in 'three to five years.' Do you remember the first night after my back surgery? We talked about our future until halfway through the night, because I could not sleep from the pain. You were sweet to stay up with me, but you told me that night you were going to be done in 'three to five years.' That was more than four years ago, Al. If you had stuck to your timetable, you'd be out by now. You have been telling yourself and me that you were going to exit from Ark sometime in the 'next three to five years' for a long time, Al."

As he listened to Valerie, at first Al felt defensive. She did not know how disruptive it could be if the company was not ready for Al's departure. Yet, she did have a point. Valerie possessed a memory like a steel trap. He could remember those conversations, too. He probably had been telling her, and himself, the same exit time frame for a while now. He was not trying to dodge the issue or stall. He had been unknowingly extending his exit, constantly rolling his timetable forward. Al was humble enough to realize his mistake on the matter, and how it was now impacting his wife.

"Okay, love," he said, reaching across the marble bar counter to take her hand. "I see your point, and you are right." Her smile immediately warmed the room and his heart. "I can't tell you right here and now when I will be done and we will sell the company. We have some important changes to make within the company before it's ready to sell."

Al could see that she was waiting for more information. "Do you remember that IT trade association conference I went to in Washington, DC, about a month ago? When I was there, I bumped into a guy I know named Ricardo Reed. He used to own an IT services company, too. Last year he sold his business—apparently for a big number. Anyway, we had dinner together one night while I was there. He gave me some great insights about what made his business more valuable when he sold it. I sat there all evening taking notes on cocktail napkins. My point is, to maximize the value of Ark, we have some changes to make."

"Big changes?"

"Not huge changes. We may be further along than many companies. For example, to sell our business for a strong price, it cannot be overly dependent upon me. Otherwise, when I leave after a sale, a buyer might be concerned about customers or key employees leaving too. Over the last few years, I have put people in place who do most of the day-to-day work. It turns out that should be good for getting a strong price and terms."

"Your business may not need you, honey, but I still do, my handsome husband," his wife said with an affectionate smile that spread across her face and into her eyes.

"Thank you, love," Al smiled back. "Getting back to business," he paused to show her that he didn't intend to talk only about business, "another strength we have is a diversified customer base, meaning we don't have a single customer that represents a big chunk of our revenues.

Ricardo, this guy I told you about, explained to me that buyers get concerned about this, again because of the risk of that one big customer leaving and causing Ark to lose all that revenue and profit. Robert and his team have done a good job creating a diverse customer base for us. This is not true for a lot of companies, either."

"Those are things that you don't need to change. So what changes are needed?" Valerie appreciated when her husband explained the business to her in detail, but right now all she wanted was to understand how long Al felt it would be before the company was ready for sale.

"Well, one change is we need to do a better job documenting our systems and processes."

Valerie's frown told Al she did not see the connection.

"We have really great people at the company, but because they are so good at what they do, we don't take the time to write down how a lot of things work, such as our customer service process, our sales methods, our training steps, and so on. When selling a business, buyers want to see that the company they're buying can be scaled up—that it could double in size in the next few years. Documenting our processes and systems makes it easier to add new people as the business expands, and this makes the company potentially more valuable. So we have work to do there."

"That's it?"

"No, there are a few other areas. We probably have to work harder growing our core business, the IT maintenance and support side of Ark. The last few years, more revenue has come from project work as opposed to our ongoing service work."

"Why is that bad?"

"It's not necessarily *bad*. The projects can bring in big chunks of cash—"

"That's not bad!" Valerie laughed, sipping more of her wine.

"No, it's not bad. Chasing project work and doing it once we get it takes resources, however. Ricardo explained to me that buyers often pay less money for project-type work because it's short-term in nature and does not happen often. The projects we do are completed in a few weeks or months, and then that customer may not have another project for several years—if ever."

"I get it," Valerie said. "Buyers prefer if the company has more 'steady Eddie' service work, rather than too many 'one-and-done' projects."

"Exactly." Al wondered why his business partner did not see this as quickly as his wife. "The project work we do has been fine up to this point, because we make some money at it and it helps customers. But when we start to look at it through the lens of what's going to maximize our value at sale, we have to be careful to not let it become too big a portion of our company."

Al popped into his mouth a thumb-sized portion of tako, his favorite. As luck would have it, right at that moment their server stopped by the table to check on them. Al used his fingers to motion for two more drinks, not wanting to speak with a mouthful of octopus.

Al could see frustration creeping onto his wife's face. Sensing that she was worried about the timing of his exit, he reassured her. "There is work to do at the company to get it ready for sale. But as I learned from this Ricardo, we are better off than many companies out there. I think we likely need one to two years to make the changes that are needed, especially with everybody at the company rowing in the same direction."

Using his chopsticks, Al picked up a piece of unagi from their shared tray and reached over to Valerie, who smiled and obligingly opened her mouth. Unagi was one of her favorites. "Love," Al said to his wife, "I agree to no more rolling 'three to five years.' Let's do this. By this summer, I will have my exit plans laid out, including a timetable for what will happen by when. We can discuss the plans over a bottle of Sangiovese in Tuscany. After all, we'll have a full month to review the plan." That, he immediately knew, was the right thing to say.

Valerie squeezed his hand, smiled, and opened the menu to see what they should order next.

Monday, about 9:15 p.m., at the Gilmore residence

Robert was tired. That morning, he arrived at Ark's offices before 6:30 a.m. as he usually did if he was in town, and after a nearly twelve-hour day, Robert had rushed from the office to attend his eleven-year-old son's soccer game. After the game he and his son grabbed takeout dinner on the way home. Now he found himself standing in a thinly lit kitchen confronted by two teenage women, asking him to referee an argument about who should get to drive the family's spare car that Friday night.

"It's only Monday," Robert Gilmore told his daughters, having to interrupt them as they debated who had the car last. "Can we deal with this another night?"

"No, Dad," both girls said in unison. The sisters' identical response seemed to make them even angrier with each other.

"We have plans to make, Dad," said Ashley, Robert's eighteen-year-old. "It's Monday already. I need the car. Lizzy had it this past weekend, so it should be mine this Friday." Ashley intentionally used the nickname her younger sister had long since ordered everybody to stop using, instead preferring Elizabeth.

Robert stuck his hands out directly in front of him like a referee dealing with an on-field skirmish. Before either daughter could continue, he said, "Enough. Not now. I just walked in the door. I am beat. We will address this tomorrow." Sensing that one or both of them might push the issue, he looked at them and sternly warned, "Anybody who mentions the word 'car' again tonight is guaranteed to be on foot this weekend." Both girls looked at him as if deciding to speak, then each other, and walked out of the room, taking care to leave through separate doorways. Robert watched them both go, wondering what happened to the two little girls who used to braid each other's hair.

Ten minutes later, Robert and his wife Tess were sitting on the couch in their family room, each sipping a glass of wine and enjoying a rare few minutes to talk. Robert could not remember taking a break all day. Tess could sense her husband was tired and sought to keep the conversation light. She told him a bit about her day up at their son's middle school, where Tess was always volunteering to help with some project or another. Sensing he was not fully listening to her, she tried to change to subject to something related to Robert's work, thinking it might engage him more. "By the way, how did Jessica do with that big sales call she had last week? I don't remember if you told me."

Robert's attention picked up, just as his wife suspected it would, and he took a sip of wine before replying. "Great from the sound of it. I did not see her at the office until today, and then we only had a few minutes to talk, but it sounded like she will get the customer. Jessica was pumped, that's for sure."

"Well, she takes after her father," Tess said with genuine flattery, but also in a further attempt to help her husband relax.

"She's not even thirty yet and she's already the company's top salesperson," Robert noted with fatherly pride. Jessica had always been a top achiever. He never expected her to come work with him, and he never presumed to ask her. Well before college graduation, Jessica had her first job lined up in pharmaceutical sales. At Jessica's graduation ceremony, Carole, Robert's ex-wife and Jessica's mother, pulled him aside and told him that Jessica only intended to work in the pharma sales job for two years so she could learn on her own how to sell. Afterwards, Jessica intended to come work at Ark. Robert was surprised to learn his daughter wanted to work at his company, but he wasn't surprised at all that Jessica laid out a plan for herself—likely a pretty good plan, at that. That was Jessica.

Remembering Jessica's penchant for setting big goals (and usually achieving them), Robert told Tess, "Jessica has never come out and said it, but I think it's pretty clear she wants to run the company one day . . . own it, too. She could do it. She's young, of course, but she certainly has the drive, smarts, and innate leadership abilities. She has time to learn and grow. I can take the time to teach her what she needs to know—it's not like I am going anywhere anytime soon."

"No, dear," Tess agreed. "No, you are not, not with three kids still yet to go to college." Tess paused and weighed in her mind if she should ask the next question. It might be too heavy of a topic for now. Yet Robert was finally smiling and pouring each of them another glass of wine, so she dove in. "When do you think you want to stop working, Robert? I am only asking because we rarely talk about this stuff. We are meeting with Shannon later this week. I always feel stupid when she asks us about our long-term goals. It feels to me like we really don't have any. It would be nice to start thinking about and planning for after you leave the company."

Robert thought for a moment. "Well, I don't have a solid date or anything, but I think perhaps in ten years I'd like to turn things over to somebody else—possibly Jessica." Robert laughed out loud. "Of course I mean Jessica. Not just because she is my daughter, either. She is the only person we have who has the potential to run the whole company someday. She'll need time to develop. I'm only fifty-two, so I am not in a rush to go anywhere myself. By then perhaps she will be running the company. At that point, maybe I will go back into sales. Whatever I do, I don't really want to retire. I just can't see myself doing nothing all day."

"What about Al?" his wife asked.

"Al? What about him?"

"Well, he's about ten years older than you, so that makes him around sixty-two, right?"

Robert nodded in agreement, so Tess continued, "Is he going to keep working another ten years too? I don't know what Al wants to do, but I can't see Valerie waiting around that long. You know she's done teaching pretty soon, and she's always talking about travel and more time away from Atlanta. It would not surprise me if they move to the beach permanently. Where does Al fit in all of this?"

His wife's questions reminded Robert how tired he was, and his early morning breakfast meeting suddenly loomed in front of him. Knowing he had to give her some answer, he said, "Sure, I can see Al being away more from the office in the future. He already rarely works past five p.m. as it is, and usually does not come in before nine in the morning, either. But I don't see Al wanting to leave anytime soon. What would he do with his time without Ark? He'd go crazy with boredom. Plus, business is great. With the amount of money we are making, he'd be crazy to want out now. I can easily see Al just wanting to hold on for the next ten years, work a lot less, and yes, likely travel more."

"Has he told you this himself?" Tess asked her husband.

"No, but that's nothing unusual." Seeing a doubtful look cross his wife's face, he explained. "Tess, we are so busy growing the business that we can't find enough time to talk about today's stuff, much less something that is likely ten years away. Al and I have been business partners for a long time. We'll figure this out when the time comes."

Tess rested her hand on her husband's neck and shoulder, a sense of concern coming over her. Seeing the need to press on, she asked, "Well, what about Jessica? If you see her getting the company one day, then what about Al? He owns half of the business. Surely he is not going to just give his half to her."

"No, of course he won't give it away. We will have to buy him out. But that's a long way away." Seeing her still concerned, he added soothingly, "Tess, it will be fine."

"It will?" she asked. "Will it go as 'smoothly' as the last time somebody was bought out?" She instantly regretted the sarcasm she let creep into her question. She reached over and caressed his shoulder in an effort to take out some of the sting. She wasn't sure how much that helped, however, because her husband gave no reply.

The couple finished their last sips of wine in relative silence. When done, Robert got up to turn out the lights and let the dog out before heading up to bed.

About two weeks earlier, 3:20 p.m.,
in Robert's office at Ark Technology Solutions Inc.

Robert sat at the small, round conference table in his office. He preferred the table over his desk when he had work that required close attention. The table was across the room, far from his phone and computer. Thankfully, reviewing Ark's latest monthly financial statements was neither onerous nor unwelcome. He found Ark to be on pace for another record-breaking year. The figures suggested that all was well in the company.

"Excuse me, Robert—do have time for a quick question?" A voice at the doorway pulled Robert's attention away from the reports, much to his relief. Robert preferred people over tables and columns of numbers. Looking up, Robert saw Reggie Chase, Ark's chief financial officer and the author of the very financial reports currently resting in his hands. Reggie stood in Robert's doorway holding a closed laptop, several files, and the mechanical pencil he was never without.

Seeing his opening, Reggie entered the office and took a seat at the small, cherry-wood table. A big man, Reggie preferred to sit whenever possible so as to not tower over the people around him. Robert knew not to be fooled by his colleague's size. Several years ago at a company bowling outing, Reggie had dazzled all of them by throwing a 240 score, displaying remarkably light footwork for his large frame.

"You asked me to forecast the growth of our cash surplus for the next twelve months," Reggie reminded his employer, opening up his laptop. "This is about hiring a project manager, right? Um, it's going to be hard for me to give you any accurate numbers at this point. I don't have the data needed to model this for you."

"Like what, Reggie?" Robert did not want to make this a big deal. "I just need to know how much we can afford to pay to a new PM without cutting into our current cash reserves."

"Yes, well, can I ask why are we hiring a project manager?"

Robert felt excited to answer that question. "To handle more of these systems installation projects we are chasing in the market. There's good work there, and profitable too. With an experienced PM, we can take on more of that work. Can't you just get me a down-and-dirty estimate, Reggie? I know you—you're great with the numbers." Robert hoped some well-deserved praise would shake Reggie loose from his typical need for precision.

"Sure, I can give you an estimate, but I could be off—way off—without good data. You said that you want to hire a PM to support more project work. Well, that project work will bring additional revenues, right? I have to take that into account to forecast cash. Those additional revenues will bring additional costs, which also have to be factored in. Nothing exists in a vacuum."

Just getting warmed up, the CFO continued. "To answer your question, I'd need to know if there would be any expected changes to our fixed costs too. To forecast cash flow, we need accurate estimates across the board for all the line items on our P&L* for the next twelve months. Once I have that data, I can get started."

"You are asking for a lot of information, Reggie," Robert observed, trying not to let his frustration show. "It almost sounds like redoing our annual budget."

"Well, in some ways, it will be. Look, Robert, we do a budget each year for the company. Then we typically file it away and don't pay too much attention to it during the year. We are pretty far into this year already, so some of that data is already out of date. If we increase our project work, that will further change our financial picture. To answer your questions, we need updated budget figures."

"Reggie, I am not against budgeting. I just tend to focus on revenue, because that's what really matters—how much money we bring in the door."

"Assuming that the revenue is profitable," Reggie gently added, in an effort to correct his boss without contradicting him. Always bigger than most other people, Reggie learned from an early age to compensate for his physical size by taking care to be gentle with others, both in body and words.

"Of course, Reggie—assuming it's profitable."

"Yes, well, either way, to get you accurate data we should update the budget. Ever since I joined Ark, we have enjoyed fairly steady growth. We have gotten by without reviewing our budget too much during the year. But budgets are not just about how to survive lean times. Budgets are also tools to help manage growth, which is where Ark is today."

Seeing no agreement to his recommendation, Reggie added, "I also think it would be particularly good for you and Al to discuss this issue."

"What do you mean, Reggie?"

---

* Profit and loss statement

For a fleeting moment, a flash of regret hit Reggie. He knew his statement could be taken the wrong way, but he was too professional to not serve the company to the best of his ability. Something needed to be said. Plus, he knew both Al and Robert were good people, both owners committed to growing the business.

Noticing Reggie's pause, Robert instructed his CFO, "Go ahead, out with it."

Reggie pulled his arms into his lap, unconsciously adopting this posture in an effort to diminish his considerable size before continuing. "Robert, I have been here for what, ten years? You and Al are great to work for. The growth we are experiencing is a lot of fun. But it's increasingly apparent that you and Al are not on the same page on some issues, including some important ones. Sooner or later that's going to be a problem."

"Okay, like what issues?" Robert had to mask his surprise. He was unused to hearing Reggie speak like this.

"Sure, take this issue," Reggie quickly answered. "You asked me last week to forecast cash flow, because you want to hire a PM to do more project work. You think there's good money to be made there."

"Yes, I do," Robert said firmly. "Do you disagree?"

"Not necessarily, but this project work is not recurring revenue, unlike our core IT services contracts. Those engagements usually last years, while these projects last months. You have said to me in the past that our margins on this project work are higher than on our service work. I don't know if that's true or not. Nobody knows at this point. We don't allocate our costs precisely between the two types of work, and so really it's anybody's guess which area is more profitable.

"This is Al's concern too," Reggie cautiously added.

"So do you and Al feel we should not do the project work?" Robert wondered what conversations had been going on between Reggie and Al without him in the room.

"No, Robert, I am not saying that. Whether we do or don't increase our project work is not my point. What I am saying is that you and Al are not on the same page. You tell me last week to forecast cash to see if we can hire somebody to help us go get more project work. Al asks me a couple weeks ago to model reducing commissions to our salespeople on the very same project-type work. Robert, I think it's pretty clear that the two owners of this company are not working from the exact same plan on how to grow this business."

"Which one of us is right, then?" Robert instantly regretted his question, knowing he sounded defensive.

"I don't think anyone is necessarily right or wrong. It's just two different ideas about the direction of this company. You two need to figure that out." Reggie paused, fearful now that he may have come on too strong. "Hey," he continued, attempting to lighten the mood, "maybe this is a blessing in disguise. Maybe now is the time to bring the team together for a discussion about this question. We don't ever really do any business planning, which has always surprised me. Perhaps this is a good reason to finally do one."

"To do one what?"

"A business plan."

Robert suspected his frustration was showing. All he wanted was to know if he could make this new hire, and Reggie was bringing up budget reviews and business plans. That would slow things down and consume a huge amount of time—time Robert felt could be spent doing more productive things.

"I think we are making this issue bigger than it needs to be, Reggie. We have not done a formal business plan at Ark in a long time—maybe never, now that I think about it. It's never seemed to slow our growth. I get that business plans are necessary at some companies, but I am not sure we need to spend time doing that here. We are in the technology industry, which changes all the time, as you know. The marketplace is highly unpredictable. New competitors pop up all the time. Plus, Al and I know this industry. Between us we have," Robert quickly did the math in his head, "something like seventy years of industry experience. I don't see much benefit in bringing everybody together for hours or even days to create some document that may be obsolete not long after we write it. Just because our ideas are not written down doesn't mean that we don't have good ideas."

Reggie wanted to point out that if all this knowledge only resided in Al and Robert's heads, the rest of the team did not benefit very much. He wanted to point out the inherent contradiction of Robert saying that the marketplace was unpredictable, but that he and Al knew the industry well. He wanted to share that planning is not about predicting the future, but rather about preparing for the future. Most importantly, he wanted to point out that no matter how good Al's and Robert's ideas were, if the two owners were trying to row the boat in two different directions, then nobody was going anywhere anytime soon.

Reggie wanted to say all of these things. However, Robert's vigorous defense of the reasons not to do a business plan cautioned Reggie against saying anything further. He did not want to upset Robert. He liked Robert and Al, and he liked working for them. They were good and smart people. They would figure this out between themselves.

"Okay, Robert, I see your points. I was only making a suggestion. So, back to hiring the PM. If you and Al would just huddle up and let me know what you decide, then I can go crunch the numbers for you. That's what you pay me the big bucks to do around here, right?" Reggie asked with an intentional dose of levity.

Sensing Reggie's effort to lighten things, Robert replied, "Thanks, Reggie. I'll get with Al as soon as I get a chance."

"When will that be, Robert? I am only asking because I don't know if I am supposed to model cash to see if can hire a PM to support more project work, or if I should model reduced commissions so our salespeople sell less project work, or both. I'll work on both if you tell me to, but then other stuff that I have to get to will fall behind. Do you and Al have a meeting anytime soon?"

"Not at the moment. You know how Al feels about meetings."

"Yeah, I do. It's the same way you feel about business plans."

Robert knew Reggie well enough to know that his CFO was only teasing. He did not find the comment funny, however, and forced a smile to hide his feelings. "Reggie, it sounds like the cash forecast is more involved than I thought and will take longer than I hoped. Plus, I don't want to tell you to stop doing something that Al asked you to do. Please continue working on both. At some point soon, Al and I will huddle up and get back to you."

Reggie gave his employer a semiofficial-looking hand salute to the forehead. The chief financial officer grabbed his laptop, files, and lead pencil, and left Robert's office. Robert watched him leave. The laptop looked more like a cell phone in the other man's giant hands. The thought made him smile, restoring some of his good mood.

Could Al really want to do less project work? That made little sense. Sure, projects did not last as long as service contracts, but Robert knew in his heart they were more profitable. Plus, just last month they picked up that staffing company as a new service customer after completing a consulting project for them. Al couldn't fathom why his partner would want to do less project work when they should be directing the maximum resources to do more.

This was always perhaps the biggest challenge with a small to midsized business, Robert reminded himself—how to sift through all the things they could do and prioritize down to the things they *should* do. Right now, Robert was behind on completing two RFPs from potential new customers, had an open marketing support position to fill, and needed to prepare for a trade show next month. He made a mental note to get with Al about this PM issue when he saw him next. In the meantime, the other, more important duties required his attention.

About ten years earlier in the conference room at Ark Technology Solutions Inc.

"Reggie Chase? Good to meet you. I'm Al Beaman," Al said, reaching upward to offer his hand. "I'm CEO of Ark Technology Solutions."

"And I'm Robert Gilmore, our VP of operations and the other owner here alongside Al." Robert also shook hands with their guest, noting how his hand seemed to disappear into the other man's. All three men then sat down at the conference table.

"Reggie, I have to say that I was worried before walking in here about Robert and me interviewing you together. We both wanted to meet you because you came so highly recommended and because, bluntly, we need someone with your financial skills. I did not want you to feel ganged up on with a two-on-one for your first interview. Now that we are meeting you, I see my worries were unfounded. Golly, you're a big fellow. I am not sure who's ganging up on who in here."

Robert cringed inside. While most people came to like and appreciate Al's frankness, Robert suspected that his business partner often gave a slightly hokey first impression.

"That's okay, Mr. Beaman. I am aware that I'm a different size compared to many other people," Reggie replied with a warm smile, pulling his arms into his lap. Robert liked this man.

"Reggie, please call me Al. I am not that much older than you. Besides, Mr. Beaman was my father, not me." Robert could see that his business partner also had warmed up to their candidate for the new controller position.

"Let's begin by telling you about Ark," Al continued. "We started this business seven years ago on a vision of doing a better job for small to midsized businesses in meeting their IT service and support needs. You see, most businesses of our typical customer's size cannot afford a professional IT support staff. Yet they also can't afford to fall behind the technology curve or have their computer and communications systems be unreliable or unsafe for lack of care and service. That's where we come in. Al and I worked together at another firm prior to starting this business, and after watching how they took care of customers, we felt like we not only could do better, but *should* do better. So, we came together . . ."

Within fifty minutes, the three men covered a lot of ground. Al delivered a compelling overview of their company, as he always did. Robert felt impressed by how thorough and organized Reggie seemed to be, diligently taking notes all through their conversation in his leather-bound notepad with a mechanical pencil. When it was Reggie's turn, he gave a confident but matter-of-fact summary of his skills and experience. Reggie was exactly what they needed. Most of his career was spent at a larger company, and he was only available because that organization was recently purchased and was potentially cutting staff. Reggie also asked a battery of insightful questions, further cementing for Robert that this was their hire. With their allotted meeting time running thin, Robert did not want the interview to end without making sure Reggie was as excited about them as they were about him.

"Reggie, before we wrap up, we'd like to tell you what makes our company special—for the right kind of person, that is," Robert said, shifting into sales mode. "We are a much smaller organization than your current employer. We like to think that employees are treated like family here. After some fits and starts in our early years, we are growing. We believe that we offer an exciting future. For that future to happen, we must upgrade our financial management team."

"By 'upgrading our team,'" Al interrupted, "Robert means it's time we got me out of paying our bills, Reggie. I don't like it, and I'm probably not the best at doing it."

Seeing the question on Reggie's face, Al explained. "Oh, I can add and subtract just fine. But really all I want to know about our finances is if we have money in the bank. If we do, then we must be okay. If we don't, then we are not. Robert says there is more to managing our business financial needs than checking to see if we have cash in the checking account or not. If he's right—and he probably is—then we need help."

Robert could see Al's self-deprecating humor having its desired effect on their candidate. He also knew, however, that there was more than a bit of truth in how Al described his financial management style. "My partner may be exaggerating a little, Reggie," Robert said good-naturedly, "but he is right that we need help. Managing our financial books and matters is not Al's highest and best use. Plus, we simply have gotten bigger and will hopefully get even bigger still, which is why we may need you."

"Yes, perhaps I can see that," Reggie replied. "Would you please tell me more about the company's current financial operations? For example, what is your process for budgeting and tracking results against plan each year?"

Al and Robert looked at each other, wordlessly determining which person should field the question. Al spoke first. "No, we don't prepare a detailed annual budget. We keep a pretty close eye on cash and receivables, though. Back when we first got started, we got off to a quick start, but then we went several years with basically no money. When you have no money, a budget doesn't tell you much, does it?"

Al laughed at his own joke. Reggie smiled politely.

"Thankfully," the CEO continued, "revenues are now steadily increasing, and profits are getting better all the time, too. Now that we have some money, we are busy talking with prospects and taking care of customers. Perhaps we may need an annual budget going forward. That could be an important part of what you do for us."

"I think it would be, Al," Reggie acknowledged. "I get it though. First you had no money, and now you have no time. We can talk specifics later, but preparing an annual budget is an important part of running a sound financial operation."

"Agreed," Robert said, glad to hear Reggie speaking as if a second meeting was a foregone conclusion.

"One more question, if I may. You both have also talked a lot about business growth. I am excited to hear about your success. Can you tell me more about where the company is going over the next several years? What are the company's goals?"

Both men again checked with each other to see who should respond. This time Robert replied. "We see ourselves growing significantly bigger over the next few years in terms of financial results and staff size. We don't have any specific numerical goals that we are aiming for—it is difficult to predict the future in the technology industry. The market opportunity for our services is large, however, and there're only a few competitors who can really do what we do."

Reggie found himself waiting for Robert to continue, and realized after a moment that there would be no more to his answer. "Um, I am sure you are right about the market potential. Is there some type of business plan that you are following that I could read after our meeting today? It would help me to know how Ark will be growing going forward, and better anticipate how my role here will support that growth—if I am hired as your controller."

Al jumped back into the conversation. "I assume your current company has some type of written business plan?" Seeing Reggie nod, Al continued. "Sure, that's to be expected—you are with a big organization. We don't do anything formal like you may be used to. Robert and I feel that's one of the advantages of our smaller size—we can be nimble and adapt quickly as the market dictates. We try and minimize things that could make us inflexible, rigid, or bureaucratic.

"For example, I am not a fan of meetings. At the company Robert and I worked at before starting Ark, we would watch people spend all day hopping from one meeting to another, never doing any real work. Made no sense to me. Around here, if people need to talk, they just grab one another and huddle up. If somebody suggests to me that we need to have a big, elaborate meeting about something, they have to prove to me why it is worth the investment before I will agree. That alone has kept meetings down to the bare minimum. In turn, everybody here stays busy working in the business, which keeps people engaged. We like to keep things simple, because it's effective. Given our growth over the last several years, it seems to be working."

Reggie recognized this was a significantly different approach than he was accustomed to at his current organization. Some of what Al and Robert said made sense, but some parts did not. For example, if the company was too small to need structured business planning, he wondered what size it needed to be before the need for formalized planning arose? Also, how did these two leaders stay aligned with one another and with their employees without some type of written document for everybody to follow?

Whatever the answers, it seemed to Reggie that Ark was an environment led by two fine men where he could make a solid contribution. The company certainly needed a controller, from what he absorbed, and perhaps one day he could be even more than a controller here. Excited by the prospect of being part of this team, he sensed they would offer him a second interview before the meeting was over.

Tuesday, 11:45 a.m., at Seasons Restaurant, Buckhead

"Hey, Linda, great to see you," Al greeted his CEO Group Chair, who responded with a warm hug. That was one of many things he liked about her. Linda could command a room full of CEOs—most of them men—to be silent and listen to her, yet still be friendly and comfortable giving colleagues an affectionate hug. Al nodded to the hostess to indicate they were ready, and she seated the pair immediately. Al knew that in fifteen minutes the restaurant would be packed with a business lunch crowd. Anybody arriving then would be waiting for a table.

Al and Linda met here almost every month, so each only needed a quick glance at the menu to know what they would order when the server arrived. Not that they were in a hurry, as they likely would occupy this table for the next one and a half to two hours. Al knew that their long lunches tied up the table and likely caused the server to earn at least one less tip during the lunch rush, so he always doubled up the gratuity. As for the restaurant, Al figured they could absorb the small loss.

Once they ordered their meals and caught up on personal matters, Linda efficiently pivoted to business mode, asking Al the same initial question she asked him practically every month for the last eight years. "Al, what is the most important thing we should talk about today?"

Al, CEO of Ark Technology Solutions, was a member of a CEO peer-to-peer roundtable group. Linda Hamill was his group's professional chairperson. Part coach, part facilitator, part shrink, and part minister, Linda helped Al and the other sixteen to seventeen CEOs in the group become better business leaders and in turn build better businesses. Al felt that outside his family, nobody knew him better than she.

In addition to a monthly full-day meeting with his group, Al attended a two-hour one-to-one meeting with Linda each month, like today's. In the beginning, Al prepared diligently for these coaching sessions, bringing issues he wanted to discuss and reports he wanted to review, all summarized in a neat agenda. Eight years later, Al just showed up to talk. It wasn't out of laziness, but a well-placed confidence that Linda would pull out of him the most important topic for them to discuss at that point in time. She was good at what she did, and he trusted her.

That did not mean Al always gave the right answer to Linda's standard opening question, at least not right away. This was one of those months. Al spent the next twenty minutes, first over a beet salad and then over an entree of Georgia Mountain trout, bringing Linda up to date about how things were going at the company. Another record sales month. Record profits, too. The sales funnel was full. Employee morale seemed good. Halfway through his trout, Al even remarked, "Gee,

Linda, this could be one of those months that we just don't have anything that we need to discuss," coming across like the kid who for the first time turned in a report card of straight As.

"That's great, Al," Linda replied, having already finished her Cobb salad while she attentively listened to Al's business review. "You and your team certainly have done a great job. Things have not always been this good for your company, so it's important to celebrate the good times and achievements."

Al smiled. Linda was not quick with praise, so he noted it when he heard it from her.

"If the present is in such good shape, then let's take the opportunity to talk about the future, Al," Linda resumed. "Where do you want to take this company? What are your long-term goals?"

"Did Valerie call you this morning and tell you to ask me that, Linda?" Al asked, not seriously suspicious. Seeing Linda's arched eyebrows, he explained. "She and I were just talking last night. Valerie is retiring in another year or two, as you know, and she grilled me pretty good last night about our future plans. She wants to travel more—a lot more. I want that, too. She and I have worked hard, and at some point I will want to move on from Ark." Pausing and carefully watching his Chair's face, he asked, "Does that surprise you? Were you expecting me to talk all about how I want to double our sales and hire another couple dozen people, and so on?"

"Why do you think your answer should surprise me?" Linda asked. In the moment, Al missed that she answered his question with a question, as she was wont to do.

"Because I have always been such a committed, hardworking person, Linda. I could never see myself not working full time, all the time," he answered. "I was quick to tell Valerie last night that I don't intend to retire in the classic sense of the word. I will always do something that challenges me and maybe generates a little income here and there. But no, I don't want to do this for another ten years and put in the same energy as before. I worked hard before starting Ark, and I've busted my butt for the last seventeen years. Now that we are doing as well as we are, I am starting to think it might be time to go out on top and move on to other things. Honestly, it surprises even me to hear myself say that out loud."

Linda listened, knowing from experience not to speak just yet and let the silence do the lifting.

Al continued. "Do you want to hear something funny? Valerie caught me last night doing something I never realized was a habit. She asked me when I would want out from the company, and I told her 'three to five years.' She then reminded me of two other times over the last few years that I gave her the same answer to that question. I never realized it until she pointed it out. Could you imagine one of my employees coming to me with some important deadline, and he or she keeps rolling the date forward every time I ask for a completion date? I'd fire that person." Al paused and checked himself. "Well, maybe I wouldn't fire somebody, but I certainly wouldn't tolerate the ever-extending deadline. Yet here I am, doing that to myself—and to Valerie." Al had not noticed, but somewhere along the way Linda started taking notes on her iPad. He waited as she finished writing, then looked up at him.

"Al, I think most business owners reach a point when, after years of taking care of their business, they start to ask how their business is going to take care of them. That's not inconsistent with being a hardworking, committed leader. I think it's human. So," she paused for a moment, "what does that mean going forward?"

To Al's surprise, his answer came quickly and clearly. "It means we sell the business," he replied.

"Okay, tell me more. What's your plan to do this?" his Chair asked.

"I don't have a plan. Before you say anything—I know, I know, I will need one. We have time to get organized. I told Valerie last night that by this summer when we go to Italy I'd have my exit all laid out."

"You're exiting by this summer?" Linda asked, hoping she did not hear what she thought she may have heard.

"That's not what I meant. I will have all my plans laid out by this summer for when we will sell the business and how that will work. I think our actual time frame to sell may be a year or two from now." Al found himself more excited to say it than he anticipated.

Linda waited to reply, carefully choosing her words. She could feel Al's enthusiasm, and did not want to come across as negative or critical. "Al, I noticed you said, 'We will sell the business.' That seems to be the right way to phrase that. What about Robert? Have you two discussed this?"

"Not in any specific way." Seeing the alarm on his business coach's face, he quickly added, "But only because we haven't yet, not because we won't, Linda. Robert and I will discuss this. I know him pretty well. I am sure he'd want to sell—for the right price, of course. He has four kids, three of whom are still young. His wife does not work out of the home, so I know what their household income is—his paycheck is the exact same amount as mine, after all. What I am saying is that he surely could use the money. Besides, we could sell for a substantial amount. Robert is ten years younger than me, so that makes him somewhere around age fifty-two. Who wouldn't want to cash out at such a young age?"

With years of experience coaching CEOs, Linda knew when to be gentle and when to take the gloves off. An image flashed in her mind of unsnapping the wrist buttons on her favorite leather gloves. "Al, Robert owns half of the company. You need to make sure he is in agreement with you about this."

"No," Al interrupted, more sternly than he intended. "He owns forty-nine percent. I own fifty-one percent."

Linda in turn interrupted her CEO client. "Are you saying you would do this over his objection, if he objected? That would surprise me, Al. Besides, I don't even know if you could legally do that even if you wanted to."

"Come on, Linda, have faith in me. I would not force this on Robert. I did not mean to imply that. I may own fifty-one percent, but he and I are partners. We run things as if it's fifty-fifty. The only reason I own the extra percent is after dealing with the issues we had all those years ago, Robert and I agreed that having a tiebreaker between us could one day be important. Being ten years older and the CEO, it made sense for me to have fifty-one percent. But no, Linda, we would decide this together."

Their server came by and inquired if Al and Linda finished their lunch. Linda's salad bowl was empty, but the second half of Al's trout was not yet touched. After politely indicating he was not finished with his meal, Al continued, "What did you mean when you said, 'Legally I couldn't sell if I wanted to'? We have a buy-sell agreement, Linda."

"Okay, well, that's good and important," she acknowledged. "Have you read it? I am not an attorney of course, but I have been a party to more than one buy-sell agreement in my day. They usually address what happens if somebody dies, but many of them don't address what happens if somebody wants to sell his or her interest in the business, beyond a first right of refusal."

"Huh? I thought buy-sell agreements are supposed to deal with issues just like these."

"You will have to read your agreement and ask your attorney," advised Linda. "In general, an agreement would need to have specific language that gives you the authority to sell all of the company stock. Without that language, you can't make Robert sell his forty-nine percent of the business just because you own fifty-one percent. I know from the companies that I once owned that this language is not as common as you might think."

"I see your point. I will make sure to meet with our attorney. He's not the same lawyer who did our agreement. I don't even remember that lawyer's name, it's been so long. Perhaps it's time to review the agreement anyway."

"That sounds like a good idea, Al," she concurred.

"I am not sure I share your concerns about Robert, however," Al said, returning to that subject. "I will talk with him of course—after I talk to the attorney. I am sure Robert would sell for the right price. Who wouldn't?"

"Somebody whose grown child is working in the business and clearly wants to be the leader of that business, that's who." Linda's gloves were fully off.

Al was never a great student in school, but what he lacked in academic accomplishments he made up for in street smarts. He was smart enough to see he dug that hole and walked right into it. Unfortunately for him, Al had a little more digging to do before he reached the bottom. "Jessica is incredibly talented, there is no doubt about that. But she's young. She could do anything in this industry. Heck, she and Robert could take some of the money from the sale and go start up a new IT company if they want. Or, a buyer would almost certainly want her as part of the deal and offer her a great job. I am sure this will work out."

Linda finished writing down a few key thoughts before replying. Al was one of her best CEO Group Members, and she considered him a friend. But he was way out front with this. She had to get some sense into him—quickly. "Al," she began, "you are going too fast and making some big assumptions. You could be right on all points, or you might not be. Let's just consider any of the other possibilities. First, Robert might not want to sell right now, at any price. He's a young guy and you both are making good money, as you said. It might take a much bigger price than anybody would reasonably pay to get him to sell his half of the company."

"Yes, but he is overpaid, Linda," Al answered, a little defensive that his vision seemed to have a possible flaw or two in it.

"That's a different issue and a separate conversation," Linda replied, attempting to stay on focus. "Robert's daughter loves that company. She may not want to leave either. It's a pretty deep emotional bond for her, and thus likely for Robert, too. Plus, your idea that they could start their own IT company after a sale likely wouldn't work. I sold my last business before becoming a Chair. While I'm not a mergers and acquisitions expert, I believe it is pretty standard procedure that a buyer is going to insist that you and Robert—and maybe Jessica—sign noncompetes as part of the sale. Those can last for several years. That would prohibit Robert and Jessica from launching their own IT company after a potential sale."

Linda paused, and made an effort to be gentler now that Al had been knocked off Mount Optimist. "Look, Al, it's great that you are committed to moving forward in a direction that excites you. That's a good thing. It's also a good thing that you and Valerie know what you want for your future. But you have got to slow down and think this through a little further. Robert could go for a sale, or he might not. If he doesn't, then where does that leave you? Are you open to Robert buying you out as a plan B? Would he want that? Do you see what I mean?"

Linda took Al's silence as a sign he was listening. To help move the issue forward, she offered Al some specific help. "I wrote down the major questions and issues that you may need to address at this point." Linda turned her iPad toward Al so he could see the screen. On it, he read:

> 1) Sell the business with Robert? To Robert? Other?
> 2) When does Al exit? On his own, or with Robert?
> 3) How much does Al need to sell for? How much would Robert sell for?
> 4) Jessica?

Reading her notes, Al appreciated yet again the power and benefit of these one-on-one conversations with his business coach.

"Okay, I get it. Would you e-mail me those notes?" Watching her click on the iPad screen to send him her comments, he continued, "I will review the buy-sell agreement as a next step. I'd like to know what it says before I speak with Robert. If the agreement needs updating, that may be an easier way to bring this subject up with Robert, as opposed to just walking in his office out of the blue and saying, 'Gee, Robert, are you ready to sell the business today?'"

As an experienced coach to business leaders and owners, Linda could tell when one of her clients was looking for a way to avoid directly confronting an issue. She would let Al get away with it, for now. She had spoken with him bluntly a couple times already during lunch. Meeting with his attorney might be an indirect step, but it was a step forward. She made another note to ask Al about his progress at their next monthly one-on-one. She also thought that Al's topic would be an excellent issue for their CEO group to discuss and process at an upcoming meeting. She'd circle back with Al on that idea later.

Lunch ended shortly thereafter after a brief joust over who would pick up the tab. Al won.

***

From day one, Linda was a diligent notetaker. The habit served her well in school, then later as a business leader and owner, and now as a Chair. Her assistant Karen carefully scheduled in Linda's calendar fifteen-minute gaps between appointments and phone calls, allowing Linda time to write down important thoughts and information and capture action items. It was not terribly comfortable writing with a stylus on an iPad screen while sitting behind the steering wheel of her BMW 6 Series, but Linda only had a few minutes before she needed to drive to her next monthly one-on-one appointment.

It was good that Al and his wife were talking about things. Linda chuckled to herself upon recalling the story Al told her about his wife catching him rolling his exit time frame forward each year. As she wrote that down, it occurred to Linda that she could think of several more business owners in her CEO groups who did the same thing in past conversations with her. Now that she thought carefully about this, she realized that lots of business owners do this—just keep rolling forward how many years from now they want to exit, without ever putting in place clearly defined goals, until they get to crunch time. This was something she needed to look into.

Al's approach to his situation concerned her. He was moving too fast, and apparently he had not spoken to his business partner about much of this, if at all. Linda also felt concerned that Al and Robert apparently were not talking about exit, and seemingly had not in a long time, if ever. Linda knew that mistake was not unique to Al, either. She mentally inventoried the CEOs and owners whom she worked with. To her surprise, more than half of her clients ran businesses with more than one owner. It would seem that the classic profile of the business owner, solitary and alone at the top, did not reconcile with reality. She strongly suspected that many of these other business co-owners also were not having the necessary conversations about exit. She made another note on her tablet.

Linda believed she had helped Al during lunch and given him sound advice. However, she also learned a thing or two herself from their meeting. She did not like that some of her other CEOs and owners could be facing the same issues as Al and possibly making similar mistakes. Before putting her iPad away, Linda made one final note. She knew somebody to call, a person who she believed could help Al, if it came to that. Having completed her notes, she hit the start button on the car's dashboard. For neither the first nor last time, the throaty rumble of the BMW's twin-turbo engine put a smile on her face. She pulled out of the parking lot, treating herself to a quick burst of speed before she knew she'd be slowed by Atlanta's ubiquitous traffic.

About sixteen years earlier, *shortly after 5:00 p.m., in Al's den, Marietta*

Al and Robert sipped their beers in silence, what little silence there was. Al's next-door neighbor was working in the yard by the sound of it, for a leaf blower's drone filled the room.

"What you think, Al?" Robert was forced to elevate his voice so his partner could hear him.

"We fight back," Al half-shouted in reply. "Protect what we've got."

"How?"

"To start, we're going to have to make some cuts—"

The leaf blower kicked into a high-pitched whine. Al recognized the sound of debris caught in its fan. A moment later the machine mercifully cut out.

"Thank goodness. As I was saying," Al continued, "we will have to make some expense cuts, based on the losses we've had already. And there could be more coming. We can't fight back if we are dead, and cash is life." Al leaned forward to grab some papers off the desk, his ancient desk chair's creaks now audible without the blower's interference. He handed Robert a handwritten list containing several of their largest customers.

Robert took a moment to review what his business partner handed him. "We have lost these accounts too? When?"

"Just in the last couple days."

"I didn't know it was this bad. He's certainly got it out for us."

Al did not see any need to comment. Actions speak loudly enough. Besides, he simply did not want to say the other man's name. Never again, if possible. Not saying his name seemed to reduce the power he had over them. He was doing enough damage as it was.

"He's calling on our prospects too, you know," Robert informed. "We've already had one that we thought was a done deal tell us that they are rebidding their work and letting him submit a proposal. They said we could resubmit ours too if we wanted, implying that we will have to cut the price that we just quoted them to have a shot now."

"I am not surprised. When he left, he knew not only all of our customers, but also all our prospects . . . and our pricing."

"We will have to make expense cuts even though we don't have to pay his salary at this point?"

"The revenue loss is already greater than what we were paying him. Robert, we also have to put back the money we took out."

Robert instantly knew Al was right, given how things stood. That did not make him dread any less the conversation he faced having with his wife. He had made such a big deal about bringing home that check, their first big profit distribution from the company. She kissed him and told him that she was proud of him. His family needed that money—still needed it. He could feel his chest tighten with worry and shame. He was letting his family down. Al's wife would be no less happy about any of this, but at least they could rely on her paycheck to fall back on.

"When we get through all of this—and we will—we will have plenty of future profits to split," Al said, sensing his partner needed a boost. Al tried to treat Robert as an equal partner at all times. However, the other man was only in his midthirties, and at critical times Robert looked to him for leadership. This was one of those times.

"Let's hope so. Plus, in the future we'll be splitting those profits fifty-fifty—when they do occur. That's something, at least."

"Absolutely," Al replied, emphasizing the positive. "We started this business as equal partners—splitting everything three ways. Well, going forward we will split things fifty-fifty: profits, compensation, benefits, all of it."

"Right, Al, I agree. But you have one percent more ownership than me and—"

"Don't say his name."

Realizing the mistake he was about to make, Robert apologized. "Sorry. You have thirty-four percent ownership, and you-know-who and I each have thirty-three percent. Hopefully we're going to get rid of this jerk and get his third of our business back. When we do, I feel you still need to have one percent ownership more than me. I have heard horror stories of people who own a business as fifty-fifty partners. They don't have any tiebreaker. That sounds like potential trouble to me.

"I trust you, Al. I know we will act as equals in making decisions, getting paid, and everything else. I think one of us needs to have a little bit more, just in case. That should be you. You're the CEO, and this company was your idea."

"By saying it was my idea, are you now blaming me for our troubles?" Al half smiled to make sure his partner knew it was a joke.

"No, I didn't mean it that way," Robert laughed. "I am serious though. Whenever we can buy this guy out, we need to end up at fifty-one and forty-nine ownership percent."

"Everything else we still split equally, though, including major decisions," Al affirmed.

"Right."

"Agreed."

"If we survive . . ." Robert said, thinking again about the conversation he would need to have at home that evening.

"We will make it," replied the CEO.

"I hope so," his partner concluded.

The leaf blower suddenly kicked back in, returning to its pre-jam drone. Both men sat in silence and drank their beers, each left to his private thoughts and fears.

Early Wednesday morning in the employee break room at Ark Technology Solutions Inc.

Reggie stood impassively waiting for the microwave to finishing heating his cup of water. He felt worthless in the morning until he downed a cup of Earl Grey tea, akin to a giant tortoise that must remain motionless until it soaks up sufficient morning sunlight. As he waited on the water, Dan Alvarez, vice president of sales for Ark, entered the break room, carrying a brown paper lunch bag. Dan opened the refrigerator and commenced the requisite game of food shuffle, the exercise that requires an employee to rearrange food in the office refrigerator, some of it long forgotten, to create room for one's newest item.

"Morning, Reggie," Dan said cheerily. "Fixing tea?" Everybody at Ark knew about Reggie's tea dependency. New employees often wondered if Reggie was of English descent.

Reggie half grumbled in greeting. Dan knew it was not an unfriendly response, but rather an energy-conservation effort on the other man's part. Dan smiled to himself, grabbed a coffee mug, and prepared a cup of coffee to meet his own caffeine needs.

Jason Lee, Ark's director of Customer Services, walked into the room exactly as the microwave timer dinged, as if on cue. "Hey, Reggie. Hey, Dan." Reggie offered another unintelligible grunt as he added a tea bag to his hot water. Dan was more vocal. "Good morning, Jason. How's customer service these days?"

"It's 'Customer Services,' not 'customer service,' thank you very much," Jason replied in good humor. He was used to Dan teasing him about his job title and knew no harm was intended. "I don't sit in a 'complaints' booth like some store clerk."

Jason nodded his head toward Reggie while asking Dan, "Not had any tea yet?"

"Gee, how could you tell?" Dan replied.

Jason moved to get himself a cup of coffee.

With all three men preparing their beverages at the break-room counter, no one noticed the woman enter the room behind them. Thus, all three jumped when a female voice shouted out, "I got it! Read it and weep!"

Reggie, Dan, and Jason turned around to see a young woman standing behind them, a huge grin spread across her face, holding some papers clenched in a fist straight over her head.

Dan bit first. "Let's hear it, Ms. Big Time. What did you get?"

"Do you three want to know? I mean, do you really want to know?"

It was Jason's turn to play along. "Yes, we want to know. Please."

"Say 'pretty please,'" she taunted.

The three men looked at each other and then turned their backs on her and resumed making their morning beverages.

"Okay! Okay! I'll tell you."

Reggie, Dan, and Jason turned back around to face her.

"Gentlemen, you are the first to lay your eyes on a signed contract with Ark's newest and perhaps biggest project ever. Closed yesterday afternoon by yours truly, Jessica Gilmore." Jessica curtsied.

The three acknowledged her with a brief but hearty round of applause.

Dan came to her to read the contract and give her a high five. "You did it! Great stuff, Jessica. You closed Magnolia!"

"You bet I did. Had to fight tooth and nail at the end, but we got it. We start work in thirty days."

"That's great, Jessica. Congratulations," Jason offered. "How was it a fight?"

"I'll give you three guesses," she replied, her playful mood turning slightly sour.

"I only need one," Dan said. "The Davidoff Company."

"Ding! Ding! You guessed correctly!" Jessica answered. She left Dan to read the contract. "That makes this victory all that much sweeter. I love beating them on a sale, because it surely doesn't happen very often."

"They are tough," Dan acknowledged. "I hate to admit it, but we probably lose to them more often than we win. It feels like they go out of their way to beat us, too. Maybe we did something to anger Kevin Davidoff in a past life."

"Who is Kevin Davidoff?" Jason asked.

"The founder of The Davidoff Company," Dan explained.

"Oh—guess I could have figured that out," Jason replied, embarrassed for not making the connection. "They are tough on us in Customer Services, too. Since I've been here, they've tried to take several customers from us, including one just recently. Just to keep that account, I was forced to go to Robert to get permission to cut our pricing. Robert agreed, but he looked like he swallowed a spider when I asked him."

Turning to Jessica, Jason asked, "So what did you have to do to beat Davidoff for this win?"

Smiling, she replied, "I guaranteed them sixty-minute turnaround time on customer service calls."

"You did what?" Jason exclaimed, horrified by her answer.

Dan and Jessica's laughter tipped Jason off. "Very funny," he replied. "I know that's the way it works with you sales people," he continued. "You promise prospects the sun, moon, and stars, and then come back and expect those of us who do the real work around here to deliver."

"Yeah, that's it. You figured us out." Jessica chuckled.

Jason joined the laughter. He liked Jessica. She could take it as well as dish it out.

Jessica turned to Dan. "Actually, Dan, if it's okay with you I'd like to present to the rest of the sales team what happened here. Our proposal had some features which proved to be important competitive advantages against The Davidoff Company. The rest of the team would benefit from seeing how we got this win."

"Of course, Jessica," Dan replied. "Great idea. Thanks for volunteering."

"Good job, Jessica," Reggie suddenly added, reaching down to give her a fist bump as he ambled past her out the door, all the while sipping his tea.

"It is alive!" Dan moaned in a B-movie monster voice. Jason and Jessica laughed even harder.

Wednesday, 4:00 p.m., in the law offices of Joseph, Cole & Wynn, Midtown Atlanta

Al stood admiring the Atlanta skyline stretched out before him. As much as he liked the view, he didn't like the thought that he helped pay for it. The lawyers at Joseph, Cole & Wynn were not the cheapest in town. Their offices on the twenty-seventh floor of a marquee tower in Atlanta's midtown district faced south, overlooking all of downtown Atlanta. Al had learned the hard way in his career that when it came to legal work, an ounce of prevention was better than a pound of cure. So he paid for good legal advice. He just wished he didn't feel like the ounces he purchased were made of platinum.

A sound behind Al alerted him to Wilson Riley entering the room. Tall, polished, fit, never in a suit without a pocket square, Wilson was the epitome of a corporate lawyer. That, however, is where the stereotype stopped. The veteran attorney was funny, easygoing, patient with his clients, and trustworthy. Al and Robert both liked him.

"Al, good to see you," Wilson walked over and shook his client's hand. Wilson grabbed a bottle of water from the side table and offered Al a cold can of soda, remembering his client's preference. Both took a seat at the sprawling, thirty-person conference table. "Sorry about the big room, Al," Wilson apologized. "Our smaller conference rooms are booked, and my office is a disaster right now. This was the only room available for us on short notice. Is it okay?"

"It's fine. Great view, so no objections."

"Good," Wilson replied. "I was glad to hear when we spoke on the phone how well business is going, and that you and Robert are both fine. I also got the copy of your buy-sell agreement that you e-mailed over yesterday. I reviewed it quickly. I presume that's what you wanted to talk about. Is everything all right? When clients want to meet on short notice, I get worried."

"Yes, Wilson, everything is fine. I had some questions about the agreement and how it works, and was hoping for quicker answers, that's all. Thanks for reviewing it." Al pulled out the hard copy he had printed before driving to the appointment. "I have some questions about what it says, and we may need to discuss updating it."

"Sure. Shoot, Al," replied Wilson. "I will say right off the bat that at more than a dozen years old, do not be surprised if it needs updating. In my experience, buy-sell agreements rarely go more than a handful of years before some changes need to be made. But let's talk about what you want to discuss."

"Okay, sure. Well, let's jump to what's at the top of my mind. When we sell Ark, can I authorize the company sale by myself, or does Robert need to agree too? Before you answer, you need to know that we don't have a buyer waiting in the wings. I just want to know how these things work before we sell the business, and before Robert and I sit down to discuss this stuff."

Wilson scribbled down some notes and pulled his hard copy of the agreement out of a leather folder. Putting on reading glasses, he flipped forward several pages into the document, scanned it quickly, and then replied, "Sure, got it. Your agreement covers many things, Al, such as if either you or Robert died, or if either one of you should want to be bought out by the other, and some other situations. Besides that, no, your agreement does not have any provisions that grant you the authority to sell the entire business without Robert's approval at time of sale. In simple words, Robert would have to agree to a sale, just like you would."

"How come our buy-sell doesn't do that?"

"It's surprisingly common, actually, for a buy-sell agreement to be missing those provisions."

Al thumbed through the document, clearly bothered by what he heard.

"Let me explain," the lawyer went on. "A buy-sell agreement is a legal document that serves to protect business owners from 'unwanted co-owners.' If my business partner dies, I probably don't want to be co-owners with his or her spouse—and the reverse. If I die, my business partner does not want to be co-owners with my spouse. Most spouses of a deceased owner don't want to get involved in the business either. So everybody is protected."

Al listened patiently, knowing Wilson would get to the part about his agreement's missing provisions.

"To do this, the legal agreement typically defines a range of situations that trigger the agreement: death or serious disability of an owner in that business, separation of employment, or the simple desire for one owner to be bought out. When one of those events occurs, the agreement's provisions kick in to protect all the parties involved."

"So our agreement covers all of those provisions, but just not a full sale?"

"Actually, no."

"What? What other provisions are not covered?"

"Your agreement does not address what happens if one owner simply wants to buy out the other owner, short of somebody dying or becoming disabled."

"Did we get a lemon of a buy-sell agreement, Wilson?"

The corporate lawyer laughed. "Well, maybe not a lemon. Somewhere around a Honda Civic."

Al's raised eyebrow indicated the need for Wilson to explain. "Your agreement has gotten you good gas mileage over the years. It's not very fancy, however, and it lacks quite a few bells and whistles."

"Okay, tell me what our agreement should have that it doesn't," Al instructed, eager to get to the issues on his mind.

"You first asked me if your agreement allows you to sell the whole company and drag Robert along as a minority owner in the sale. As I said, your agreement does not have this provision, and unfortunately that is the case with many buy-sell agreements that I see. The provision in question, by the way, is typically called 'drag-along-tag-along.'"

Al looked up from his notes, not sure if he heard his lawyer correctly.

Seeing Al's questioning look, Wilson repeated himself. "Yes, that's right. Drag-along-tag-along. This provision binds multiple owners together if selling the business to a third-party buyer. The 'drag-along' part requires that if the majority owner—that's you, of course—sells his stake in the business, the minority owners—Robert, in this case—are required to join the deal. This protects majority owners against minority owners encumbering a sale. Tag-along is the reverse, as you likely can guess. With a tag-along proviso, the majority owner cannot sell his or her stake without the minority owners tagging along and being included at the same price and terms. This protects minority owners from being left out of any deal.

"Your agreement does not have a drag-along-tag-along provision. Therefore, you cannot compel Robert to sell his interest in Ark. He is free to sell or not sell if a third-party buyer comes along."

"Am I right in assuming no buyer is going to want just fifty-one percent of the business?"

"It is *possible* to find a buyer for just your fifty-one percent," Wilson replied. "I would say unlikely, however. It certainly greatly diminishes the pool of potential buyers. Plus, Robert can likely slow or block any deal by simply being uncooperative with the potential buyer for your fifty-one percent. I am not saying he would do that; I am saying he could."

"Meaning, I can't sell unless we both completely agree?"

"Practically speaking, yes, that's true." Wilson let that sink in, then continued. "Want to tell me what's on your mind regarding this? You and Robert have always led the business more as equal partners than anything else. I see fifty-one and forty-nine ownership situations from time to time, but you two run your business as equal partners. Has there been a change in your relationship?"

"No change. Selling a business would be a joint decision," Al answered. "At least I would want it to be a joint decision. I have been thinking back to why we set things up as fifty-one percent owned by me, forty-nine percent owned by Robert. We did that because I am about ten years older, and I am more the face of the company, whereas Robert is more the day-to-day side of things. We also felt that a tie-breaking vote was prudent. Now you are telling me we don't have that. You are saying that I can't sell my portion of Ark if Robert vetoes it."

"Having a fifty-one and forty-nine ownership structure can make a lot of sense for many business decisions, Al. As you said, every now and then you might just need a tie-breaking vote as you run your business. But running a business and selling a business are two different things. Without drag-along-tag-along provisions in the buy-sell agreement, then minority owners can hold up any deal from happening—not for any legal reasons, but simply because the marketplace usually prefers a clean deal with all owners in alignment."

Al sat still, saying nothing. Wilson could see his client was processing this new perspective and gave him the time.

"In some ways this does not change much," Al said with a sigh. "I mean, I fully intended to discuss selling the business with Robert and securing his agreement. I guess what changes is that I *must* get him to agree, as opposed to it being really nice if he agreed. Do I have that right?"

"Yes."

"What if he does not want to sell the business?"

"You have a range of options in that situation. You could simply not sell—"

"Ever?"

"Well, at least not right now. Sooner or later you will exit from your business—both of you. Death is not an exit strategy, Al."

Al laughed. "No, death is not a strategy. For me, doing nothing is not an option either. I am not going to hang around indefinitely. I don't want that, and I would not do that to my wife, Valerie."

"Okay then, if Robert does not want to sell his interest in Ark, then your remaining options would be to buy out Robert so you can then sell the entire business, or Robert will have to buy you out."

"Tell me about how our buy-sell agreement addresses those options," Al asked, motioning to the agreement laid out on the table before him.

"Your agreement has some provisions to help with this, but it lacks some as well. The agreement has language that says if one of you wants to sell to the other, you will need to agree upon a price. If you cannot agree upon a price, then you each get a valuation to determine that price. This approach is quite conventional. However, under your agreement all of this is still voluntary. Nobody can make the other person buy or sell. You both must still agree to a transaction."

"So in essence, even with those scenarios, Robert still has a veto over my exit?"

"Technically yes, you can describe it that way. But let me put it another way. You and Robert co-own a business together, right? In my experience, most of the time business co-owners need to work together to figure out a mutually agreeable exit plan. One owner usually cannot just force his or her needs on the other, not without undesirable consequences.

"Now, you would have the ability to force a sale if your buy-sell agreement had a 'shootout clause' provision. This—"

"Wait, a *what*?"

"A shootout clause."

"Wilson, I never knew the legal community had such funny names for its concepts."

"The names for some of these things may be uncharacteristically comedic," Wilson acknowledged, "but the provisions play a serious role. Under this provision, if one owner wants out but the other does not, then the provision forces a showdown that leaves only one owner standing. This avoids a messy fight over how much the business is worth.

"It works like this. Let's say Owner A wants out of the business, but Owner B does not. Under this provision, Owner A would submit an offer to sell his interest in the business to Owner B at a specific price and under specific terms. Owner B would then have a defined period of time to accept the offer and buy out Owner A at that price and terms. If not, then Owner B must sell out to Owner A under identical price and terms. The owner making the initial offer to sell his interest is not going to set the price too high, because the other owner could turn around and sell his stake for that high amount.

"The shootout clause usually is written to also apply if one owner wants to buy the other out, and then the process works in reverse. Either way, when the dust settles, there is only one owner left standing. The two owners may not be happy with each other afterwards, but they have avoided getting into a dispute where the only one who wins is me."

"You?"

"Yes—me. The attorney," Wilson explained, a good-natured smile on his face.

"Oh, right, sorry. I get it," Al replied. "I guess I don't think of you as an attorney."

"Gee thanks, Al."

"So, am I correct in assuming that our current buy-sell agreement, lacking these provisions, doesn't really help us in terms of figuring out my exit strategy—or *our* exit strategy?"

"It's not worthless, but it lacks some provisions that would be prudent for business co-owners to implement up front, long before anybody wants to sell."

"I see. We did not do that." Al thought for a moment before he continued. "It's not as simple as just implementing a new agreement, is it?"

"I would agree that you and Robert need an updated agreement for the reasons we discussed, but also because there are a few other provisions that we have not talked about which you two should consider. We can go over those if the three of us sit down together. As you know, I am Ark's attorney and represent both of you together. To answer your question, however, no, it's not as simple as just implementing a new agreement. If you and Robert were presented with a new agreement, Robert would rightly and understandably want to know about these new provisions—what they are, and why you are suggesting they be added into the agreement. I'd like to take your money, but before I could start drafting a new agreement, you and Robert should have a conversation."

"An honest lawyer?" Al asked with a smile. Wilson never minded the teasing. He was often the first one in the room to point out his profession's occasionally negative stereotypes.

"Look, Al, talk with Robert. I understand your frustration—the buy-sell agreement leaves some things open and unaddressed. That could make things harder somewhere down the road. If we were starting from scratch, we'd do it a little differently. But you are where you are. You and Robert have a good relationship. Your path to a happy exit is not through a legal document, it's through an aligned approach with Robert."

"Thanks, Wilson. I hear you."

"Before you go further, I know an investment banker for you to meet. His name is Taylor Collins. He is sharp and with a good firm. I have worked on a few deals with him. One of them actually was another IT services company, so he knows your industry. Taylor can tell you and Robert what Ark might be worth at sale in today's marketplace."

"Do you know what he charges for doing that?"

"He likely won't charge anything. I'm not suggesting you get a formal appraisal of the company. That costs money. Rather, you and Robert want him to provide a rough estimate of Ark's market value. You'll need to provide him with your financial statements. He'll do this for you because it's only a couple hours of research on his part, and you're a prospect for him. I'll have Taylor give you a call, if you have no objection."

"Sure, that's fine, Wilson. I will be glad to talk with him." Al sat quietly for a moment longer, then stood up. "Send me a bill for this soda. I am sure it's going to be a costly can." Al shook Wilson's hand, glad for the other man's time and help.

Thursday, 9:45 a.m.,
at the offices of Stewart Wealth Management, LLC, Dunwoody

"So, that's generally where things stand in your overall financial picture. Your investments are up for the most part, your kids' college savings accounts are growing nicely, and your insurance coverage seems to be fine at this point. I think today we shared a really good discussion about your long-term retirement goals too, maybe for the first time in the five years I have worked with you. Overall, I'd say things look pretty good."

Shannon Stewart closed her copy of the bound report in front of her. The front cover read "Gilmore Financial Review" in gold, embossed letters. An identical copy sat in front of Robert and Tess Gilmore. Shannon, in her midforties, was young enough to embrace technology but experienced enough to appreciate the value of professionally printed and bound reports for her clients. At last year's annual review, Tess remarked that she and Robert saved every report Shannon prepared for them, confirming the financial advisor's methods.

"Thanks, Shannon," Tess said. "We appreciate these reviews. Robert handles our day-to-day financial affairs, so it means a lot to me to get a detailed report on how things are doing once a year. I have a few female friends who have practically no idea about their family's personal finances. There is no way I would sleep at night doing things that way." She reached over and took her husband's hand into hers.

"Every married couple is different, in my experience," Shannon replied diplomatically. "However, I understand your point. I would never condone one spouse being in the dark about financial matters, regardless of gender. My husband leaves most of our financial matters to me. It is what I do for a living, after all. We sit down once a year, though, and go through the same review I just took you through.

"Before we wrap up, is there anything else you wanted to talk about?"

"Yes, actually," Robert replied. "I would like to go back to the estate-planning section of the financial plan. You said that our estate planning looked pretty good for now, but then said we might need to do something about it before too long. Can you explain what you meant?"

"Sure. You two are, right now, at an in-between stage, between accumulating money for retirement and considering gifting some away for estate planning."

"You want us to give away some of our money?" Tess asked, barely beating her husband to the question.

"Well no, not yet, at least." Seeing the question on her clients' faces, she explained. "Your net worth is increasing each year, especially the estimated value of your half of Ark, Robert. That's a good thing, of course. However, based on your net worth and how fast it is growing, at some point we may have to be more aggressive about addressing potential estate taxes. You are both in your early fifties, so you are young—"

Valerie looked at Tess, expecting her comment to please the other woman. It did.

"—Young enough that typically we are only focused on accumulating wealth at this stage in your lives. Most people don't have the size of net worth that you do, however, and it is increasing. If that growth continues without doing anything about it, you could wake up in your seventies and eighties with a substantial estate, only to find that your heirs face a large potential tax bill. I don't know about you, but I feel my clients have worked too hard to see a third to a half of what they have built go to estate taxes when they die."

"Tess and I don't want that either. But, we also don't want to leave so much to our kids that they never have to work."

"That's how most of my clients feel, Robert. The easiest solution to the future potential estate-tax problem is to not wait until your older ages to do anything about it. Instead, we want to slow down the growth of your taxable estate. Notice I did not say we slow down the growth of your assets. We want your assets to increase in value. I *did* say we slow down the growth of your taxable estate. The most common way to do this is to take assets that you own and get them out of your taxable estate. That means giving them away.

"That does not mean," the financial planner said emphatically, "that this strategy involves writing checks to your kids. It more commonly means setting up trusts for your kids, and moving assets into those trusts so that one day those assets will pass to your children and potentially grandchildren estate-tax free. Most parents set the trusts up in such a way that their children and other heirs cannot access the money without a good reason, or until the children are old enough to make mature choices. Keep in mind, I am giving you the shortened explanation of how this works.

"Doing all of this may still be a few years away for you. However, if Ark keeps growing like you tell me it is, then we may need to consider some of these estate-planning strategies soon."

Robert turned directly to her and said, "Shannon, we are having a great year at my company and doing our best to accelerate the business's growth. I'm trying to hire another key position right now just for this reason. Knock on wood, but our net worth should increase even faster going forward."

"In that case, Robert, this may be the time to consider a gifting strategy as part of your estate planning." Shannon made a series of notes in the margin of her report copy.

Tess waited for the other woman to finish writing. "Shannon, am I hearing you say that the faster Robert's company grows, the more we pay in estate taxes? No wonder so many people who own a small business vote conservatively," Tess observed.

"Politics aside," Shannon diplomatically replied, "yes, that's potentially correct."

"So, when you talk about gifting assets to our children, what assets are we talking about? There is not a long list of choices," Robert observed.

"That's right, in your situation there are not a lot of assets to choose from. Your wealth, like most business owners, is largely concentrated in your company. Typically, we don't gift your cash or home—"

"Glad to hear that," Tess remarked.

Shannon laughed. "Most clients are. You should not give away the assets you will need to support your lifestyle, such as your primary residence and the investments needed for income. Also, even if a person has surplus cash—which you do not—gifting cash is not desirable for another reason. The ideal assets to remove from your taxable estate are those which are likely to appreciate in value over time. Cash typically does not appreciate.

"Here's the reason why: When you gift an asset out of your estate, you are removing from your taxable estate not only the present value of that asset, but all future growth of that asset as well. Let me give you an example. Assume I have two assets, both worth one hundred dollars today, and I am considering gifting them to reduce the size of my taxable estate. The first asset is likely to be worth one hundred and five dollars in a few years. The second asset I expect to be worth one hundred fifty dollars after the same period of time. It's far better to gift the second asset, because I will have removed one hundred fifty dollars from exposure to taxes, rather than just one hundred and five dollars. Does this make sense?"

"Sure," Robert replied, seeing that his wife was following too. "Why not gift everything out of the estate then—other than our home and the investments that we need for retirement?"

Shannon nodded, expecting the question. "Well, in some cases that does happen. But there are limits to how much a person can gift without triggering the very taxes we are working to avoid. Again, I am paraphrasing how estate and gift taxes work, but this is a broad explanation."

"I think I can see where this is going," Robert remarked. "Probably the best asset we have to consider gifting out of our estate is my ownership in the company. It's very likely to appreciate in value—at least we hope it will. Because we don't gift away our home or our investment nest egg, there's not much else left to consider gifting anyway, right?"

"That's exactly right," Shannon replied. "Robert, doesn't your daughter Jessica work with you? Is it possible she will follow in your footsteps and one day be the next owner of Ark?"

"Yes, that's probably what Jessica wants. We would want that for her too. It won't be as simple as that, though," Robert said, nodding to his wife. "Tess and I have three children of our own—Jessica's half sisters and brother. We can't just give Jessica my stake in the company without considering the three other children. Plus, we will need some money from the company for our retirement when that day comes. We can't just give it all to her, even without taking into account the other kids."

"Exactly," said the financial planner. "That's what I meant when I said you two were 'in between.' You are too young to be giving away large parts of your estate just yet, but your estate is already fairly large by most people's standards, and as you said, your largest asset is growing at a fast rate. Based on these numbers, it might make sense to meet with an estate-planning attorney to explore giving your oldest daughter some of the business sooner rather than later."

Robert took the time to make several notes to himself in the report Shannon prepared for them. While he wrote, Tess asked, "Can we talk about all of the kids for a minute and our estate planning? If we give some of Robert's half of the company to Jessica—and maybe one day all of it to her—what do we do about treating fairly the three children we have together in our marriage?"

Shannon was expecting this question to come back up. "As for your three other children," she explained, "that is another issue business owners face with their estate planning. The issue is how to treat all of your children fairly, even though only some work in the business and some do not. The business is your largest asset. Businesses don't divide up well between siblings. In your situation, if you just split up your ownership of Ark into four equal parts—one for each child—that likely would not work."

"No, that would not be fair to Jessica," Tess said. She respected and acknowledged her stepdaughter's role in her husband's business.

Shannon nodded in shared recognition. "When it comes to passing down a family business to children, 'equal is not fair and fair is not equal.' How to treat your children fairly is an important topic, and one that often does not have an easy solution. It may not be something you have to worry about just yet, however. Thankfully, you both have many years before your estate will be divided up among your children. Should something awful happen to you, Robert, at a younger age, then under your buy-sell agreement with Al, Tess would be bought out by Al, leaving you mostly with cash. That removes the challenge of how to figure out splitting up your estate. Cash is much easier to plan around than a small business."

"So you are saying that if I die anytime soon," Robert said with a sardonic laugh, "the problem of splitting up my estate among all four of my children goes away? That's reassuring."

"Yes, that one specific problem would likely go away. You're not likely going anywhere anytime soon, however. I am sure Tess and the kids will be glad to have you stick around for a while."

Tess squeezed her husband's arm in agreement with their financial planner.

"You probably have time to figure out the issue of treating your kids fairly in your estate planning. What may not be able to wait, however, is taking some action to slow the growth of your taxable estate as we discussed earlier. This may need to happen sooner rather than later. Gifting some of your ownership to Jessica would be an important option to consider."

Robert and Tess sat quietly, holding hands.

"Let me ask you a question related to this. Would your business partner have an objection to you giving some of your stock to Jessica?"

Tess looked at her husband, curious to hear his answer.

"I don't think so. I can't see how he would not know that's what I intend to do. My daughter is already a top salesperson for us, not to mention a natural leader. I think everybody can see that she is the future of our company once she's had more time and experience."

"Okay. If you intend to pass your share of the company to Jessica, then what is Al doing with his half? Are you buying him out? Is Jessica?"

"We have not figured that out yet, but we will. We have time. You don't know Al. He's easygoing and not working as hard as he once did. I am sure he'll be happy to ease back over the next five to ten years, let Jessica continue to develop, and figure out what we do for him."

Robert's answer made Shannon slightly concerned for her clients. "Sure, Robert. You and Al may want to map some of this out relatively soon, though. I am not specifically trained in exit planning. However, I have worked with enough business owners to know the importance of getting co-owners on the same page. This is exactly what my father went through after I came to work with him."

"Really?" Tess knew nothing about the firm's history, she realized.

"It's a long story, which I would be glad to tell you sometime. The short version is my father had a partner when I started working here. His partner wanted to eventually sell the business, but my dad wanted me to have it one day. After a lot of challenges, we eventually agreed that I would buy out the former partner. It took me years to make the payments, and the taxes were a bear."

Robert thought about all of this for a moment. "Thanks for everything, Shannon. As you said, we have some work to do at Ark. The good news is we are blessed with a strong and growing business; we have time to figure this stuff out."

Shannon rose in recognition of the closing of their meeting. "Just don't wait too long to figure this out between you and Al. The way the taxes work, as the value of your company grows, the taxes to pass your ownership to Jessica potentially grow, as well. If you intend to pass your interest in the company down to your daughter someday, the sooner you and Al are in alignment, the better."

Robert rose, shook Shannon's hand, and readied himself to leave. He wondered how sure he was about Al's feelings on these matters. He thought Al would go along. Al would like the idea of working a little less each year as he and Jessica took over more leadership in the business. They'd have to figure out his compensation, of course; if his workload fell significantly, at some point Al's comp would have to be reduced, too. But after all these years of splitting everything equally, Robert knew Al to be a fair person. Robert and Jessica would not be hardnosed about that. There was plenty of time to work this out.

Robert turned to see if his wife was following. Tess and Shannon were comparing photos of their children, passing smartphones back and forth and laughing over the quick stories they shared. Robert picked up his wife's jacket and waited patiently until she was ready to leave.

About one month earlier, 5:20 p.m., Washington, DC

Al welcomed the walk back to his hotel from the convention center, despite the evening's chill. Having grown up in the Midwest, the way his blood thinned since living in the South for the last thirty years surprised him. After a day of shuffling from general sessions to breakout workshops, sitting in quasi-comfortable chairs and staring at a seemingly endless stream of PowerPoint slides, it felt good to be outside stretching his legs.

He did not always attend this particular trade association's annual conference, but he tried to attend at least one industry event every year. Al believed in lifelong learning. Being in the technology services industry, there was always something new to learn. With more than forty years of experience, however, he often had to sit through two or three days of sessions before he heard a new idea or kernel of information impactful to his business. Thankfully, one gem could make the investment of attending the conference worthwhile.

A day and a half into this event, he didn't have his gem yet. The workshops so far proved adequate, and he collected a stack of handouts to bring back to various people on the Ark team, but no diamonds or pearls just yet. Al checked his watch as he walked, conscious of the time. He was scheduled to meet Ricardo Reed back at the hotel for a beer and was looking forward to their conversation. Al only learned that Ricardo was a speaker at the conference when he checked in at registration and received the breakout session schedule. Upon this discovery, Al immediately noted the session time and room.

When the time for Ricardo's session arrived, Al got to the assigned room early and took a seat in the front row. Ricardo saw him before the workshop started and waved hello from the podium. It wasn't Ricardo's topic that intrigued Al—maximizing employee engagement in your IT firm, although Al did pick up a few things during the presentation. Al was highly curious to learn about Ricardo's sale of his business.

Ricardo and Al served together for several years on the national membership committee for this same trade association, both men taking turns chairing the group. Al learned to respect his colleague's accomplishments, for Ricardo built a highly successful IT business out of Dallas, Texas. Al was surprised to hear several months ago that his friend sold his company. Getting close to the hotel now, Al checked his watch again. He wanted to stop by the hotel room, drop off his briefcase stuffed with handouts, and call Valerie before meeting his friend in the hotel lobby bar.

Twenty minutes later, Al located Ricardo in the bar sitting alone at a tall table near the window overlooking Massachusetts Avenue, in front of him a glass of beer already down by about half. As Al walked over, Ricardo stood and offered him a warm, double-handed handshake.

"Is this what the future has in store for me?" Al motioned to the partially consumed beer.

"What do you mean, my friend?" Ricardo gestured for Al to sit down.

"I mean that I'm five minutes early, but you are already here and well into a beer. Is this a small insight in the life of recreation and relaxation which you are living, now that you have sold your company?"

Ricardo laughed, revealing a big, natural smile. Al observed that his friend certainly looked happy.

"I don't know about that, my friend. I certainly am not filling my days drinking beer. But, yes, I do have more freedom and less worries now than I perhaps once did. I must admit, so far it suits me."

A server came by and Al ordered a draft beer too. "Ricardo, please don't take me as selfish. I want to hear all about you and your family. I admit, though, I am eager to hear most about the sale. I have a hundred questions. I am sure some things you maybe can't say, but whatever you can tell me, I will be a sponge. Most importantly, I hope you are happy. It certainly seems like you are."

"Thanks, Al. I am happy. I appreciate you saying that. And you can ask me anything you want—glad to you tell what I can."

The two men spent the next half hour talking about the sale of Ricardo's business. Ricardo did most of the talking, answering all of Al's questions. Halfway through, Al grabbed his cocktail napkin and took a few notes on it. Ten minutes later, he grabbed Ricardo's napkin after his was covered.

Halfway through a second round of drinks, Al observed, "Ricardo, what surprises me is how much the potential buyers asked you about before making their offers, and then how much more you had to cover during due diligence. Admittedly, I've never sold a business before, but I thought the process largely focused just on a company's financial results."

"Yes, Al, buyers want to know as much as they can. It surprised me too about the depth and breadth of questions they asked and information they wanted. They went well beyond our financial results. My investment banker put it this way—'Buyers want to know not only how much your company did, but also how your company did it.' It turns out, my friend, that there are a lot of ways to grow a company, but some of those ways translate into value at sale and some do not."

Al did not expect to hear this. "Can you give me an example, Ricardo?"

"Sure. One thing the buyers wanted to know about was me. How important was I to the company? Why was I selling? Buyers wanted to understand my role and responsibilities in the company, and how dependent the company was on me. Lots of small- to medium-sized businesses cannot do much without their owners. The owner may be the business's top salesperson, or have the key customer relationships, or perhaps is the most knowledgeable and experienced employee at whatever the business does. Sometimes, the owner is simply the glue that holds the company together through his or her leadership presence. Any of those things can and likely will reduce the business's value at sale. If the business is dependent on the owner, then the value walks out the door when the owner does."

"Ricardo, I suspect your company was fine there. You built a strong team underneath you, from what I saw."

"Yes, we had good answers to those questions, I am pleased to say. From what I know about Ark, you too have a strong team within your organization."

"I think so," Al replied. "I hope buyers will agree."

"They likely will in your case, Al. You'd be surprised, however. I have learned that many owners do not have a company that can survive without them. To sell for maximum value, ideally the company cannot only survive without the owner, but can actually thrive without the owner after his or her exit."

"What else did you learn that I should know?"

"A lot, my friend. There's a long list of things that potential buyers want to understand about the business beyond its financial results. I think that's why due diligence takes months, not minutes. Somebody with a good head for numbers can discern within a relatively short time how much sales and profits a company did in recent years. Buyers then take a couple months to verify those numbers, and dig deep into all the stuff behind the numbers that increases or decreases the business's value to them.

"Customer concentration is another big issue. Lots of businesses can grow every year and make a lot of money from one or two large customers. This feels good along the way, but at sale it actually presents risks to buyers. Our potential buyers asked a lot of questions about our customer mix. I was glad to show them that our largest customer was less than two percent of total sales. The company that eventually bought us told me several times how important this was for them, because many of the companies they look at will have ten, twenty, sometimes thirty percent or more of revenue from one customer. Buyers pay less for companies with customer concentration, or don't buy them at all."

Al briefly got up from the table, walked over to the bar, and grabbed a small stack of cocktail napkins. Ricardo laughed upon his friend's return. "I wish the people in my breakout session took as many notes as you are tonight, Al."

"Sorry, Ricardo. I am not trying to be obnoxious. It's just that you offer great information. I want to get it all. Eventually I'll need to share this with my business partner, Robert Gilmore."

"It's no problem, my friend. I am flattered you are interested."

"What else was important to buyers?"

"Let's see . . . I just talked about customer mix, so let me talk about revenue mix. Buyers usually want to see recurring revenue, rather than nonrecurring revenue. It's more stable and less risk for them. Thankfully our company was strong in this area too, although purely by accident, I must admit. Over the years, we saw our competitors landing large projects from customers: new system installations and upgrades, feasibility studies, consulting projects, and so on. We tried to get our share of that work, but for whatever reason, we never had much success. So we gave up chasing it. As a result, when I sold, our revenue mix was almost entirely recurring revenues from long-term service contracts, with very little nonrecurring revenue coming from one-off projects. This turned out to be advantageous. Buyers want the predictability and security of recurring revenue, especially if there is a legal contract with the customer which includes language permitting assignability or transferability. In some industries, by their very nature it is difficult to create recurring revenues. In our industry, as you know, we can grow our companies through either method, but buyers put more value on recurring revenues. It's another example of how growing a business and creating value are not necessarily the same thing."

Al continued writing for a moment, then took another sip of his beer. Putting his pen down, he looked up at Ricardo. "That one may hurt us a bit. We have a strong book of service customers. However, over the last few years we've grown enamored with these projects, just like you talked about. Our salespeople like selling them because of the big commissions, our operations people find the work fun and glamorous, and our financial people like the big cash infusion. Not to be crude, but this stuff is like crack. On a percentage basis, project work has become a large share of our revenue mix, and I am afraid it's growing faster than our service business. You're telling me that's bad."

"Are you asking me if crack is bad?" Both men laughed. Ricardo continued, "I am not saying the project work you are doing is bad. I am saying it's not as valuable to buyers as recurring revenue. If you pick up a few projects here and there, that's great. Do them. Make money, my friend. Just don't fall into the trap of equating that activity with increasing the value of your business at sale, because it may not."

Seeing consternation on his colleague's face, Ricardo asked, "Al, should I infer that you are considering selling your business?"

Al surprised himself with his answer. "Yes. At some point, yes, I'd like to sell. I don't know when or for exactly how much, but I don't want to die in the saddle. I also don't want to be financially dependent on my business forever, either. So at some point I'd like to exit, and for me that means a sale."

"I felt the same way, Al, before finally deciding it was time. I am glad that I took the time to get prepared the right way. I didn't just jump when some offer came along. More often than not, that is a mistake."

"From what you have already told me, we have work to do, especially in this area of revenue mix. Better to know now when I can do something about it, right?"

"That's right, my friend," Ricardo replied.

"Hey, I am being rude. Are you hungry? Can I buy you dinner? I owe you big time for all you have shared with me. I could go home right now and this trip is already a gold mine for me."

"Sure, sounds good. Let's just stay here and order something. If you don't run out of napkins, there's more I can share with you. You've been my best audience of the day."

"If I am not imposing, that would be great, Ricardo. Let me find a hostess and get us some menus."

Ricardo and Al spent the next couple of hours talking over dinner about Ricardo's experiences selling his business. Ricardo explained the importance buyers place on having well-documented processes and systems in order to make the business more scalable. He walked Al through the need to have a credible written business plan, to show potential buyers a clear path for sustainable double-digit business growth. He explained the importance of creating a compelling brand and reputation strategy, and building a portfolio of defensible and valuable intellectual property assets. Soon, another half dozen napkins spread across the table, covered with Al's scribbled notes.

As promised, Al picked up the dinner tab, assuring his friend that it was some of the best money he ever spent. As dinner concluded, they caught up on personal and family news, and parted with a warm handshake and commitment to stay in touch.

As Ricardo walked away, Al made one more note in the remaining space of his final napkin: to find out what his friend liked to drink other than beer, and then send him the best bottle of that libation. Folding the napkins into a careful wad, he headed for the elevator, unable to get out of his head the realization that although they were doing a fine job growing Ark, growing a business and creating value are not the same thing. He needed to find some time to share all of this with Robert. There was work to be done.

Friday, 7:30 a.m.,
in the offices of Ark Technology Solutions Inc.

Jason Lee wiped the sweat from his palms on his pants one last time before walking down the hall to Robert's office. As expected, Robert could be found already working at his desk. After a year and a half working for Robert as the company's director of Customer Services, Jason knew his boss to be an early bird. Jason intentionally scheduled this meeting early in the morning, before most of Ark's other employees would arrive.

Robert must have sensed his presence. Before Jason could knock or say anything, Robert looked up, smiled, and motioned him in.

"Good morning, Robert," Jason said pleasantly to start things off.

"You too, Jason. Happy Friday as well."

Robert seemed to be in a good mood. He usually was, but today was important. Without waiting for a cue, Jason moved to take a seat at the small conference room table in Robert's office. Jason and his wife Kim discussed beforehand where he should sit. She recommended the round table. With both men seated at the small table, it conveyed a sense of equality. Kim also role-played with him half a dozen times what he would say. Kim being involved in preparing for this meeting was necessary. Not only was this their family's future, she was also bankrolling him.

Robert noticed Jason seating himself at the small table and moved to join him. "Jason, how are we doing with Asperon these days? Any issues?"

Jason expected Robert to jump into some topic when their meeting began, even though it was Jason who scheduled the meeting and therefore presumably would have set the agenda. Jason deftly delivered his wife's suggested response. "They are fine. There are a few things about their account we could talk about later today, if you like. But there's a different topic I'd like to discuss with you this morning, if you have no objection."

Jason could see surprise—and curiosity—register on Robert's face. "Sure, Jason. That's fine. It's your meeting. What's up?"

Jason made a mental note to score one for his wife. "Thanks, boss. I appreciate the time this morning." Palms already sweaty again, he delivered his carefully rehearsed opening. "I wanted to talk with you this morning about my future here. Since you hired me eighteen months ago, results in the Customer Services department have significantly improved. They were already good," Jason was careful not to disparage the past because Robert had managed customer services before hiring him, "but now they are even better. The customer retention and satisfaction numbers show this. We also now have a good team underneath me—one that can drive the company's growth. I am happy here, and paid well for my position. However, I want to be an owner in a company, and I'd like that to be here. I want the opportunity to buy into Ark."

Jason stopped and waited. Kim and he agreed that it would be important to gauge Robert's initial reaction before saying too much. Robert sat rather still, legs crossed and arms folded over his knee. The silence seemed intolerable to Jason. Finally, Robert spoke. "Jason, it sounds like you have given this some thought. Please continue."

Neutral. That was how Jason would later explain his boss's initial reaction to Kim. Robert did not give him a clear reaction in any direction. So, he proceeded to his second planned statement.

"Yes, I have given this some thought. I am happy here. I would like to be here for the long-term. I can continue to add value as a leader in the company. I am only thirty-three years old, but I already have more than ten years' experience in technology services. I have excellent relationships with the customers and my services team. I believe the other employees like me and respect me, including Jessica."

Jason immediately noticed a change on the other man's face.

"I agree with your assessment of your results so far here, Jason," Robert said. "I also agree that you are widely liked and respected. Why did you mention Jessica in particular, though?"

"Well, because she is your daughter. I have not spoken with anybody about my desire to be an owner here until right now. Jessica has never said anything to me either about her future. But I suspect that, as your daughter, she will likely be an owner here one day. She certainly is talented and hardworking. The way I see it, she is not going to leave us, and I can't see her working here for her entire career and not becoming an owner at some point. Plus, she's in sales. My role is in Customer Services. There's a complementary skill set between us."

"Okay," Robert hesitated momentarily. "I get it. Proceed. I interrupted you, Jason."

Jason made an in-the-moment decision to drop the rest of his second planned statement and jump ahead to the "pitch," as he and his wife called it. "I don't know anything about what you and Al have in mind for your futures and the company. Al is older than you, however, so I suspect that he may want to retire before you do. I believe I can be an excellent leader and owner, alongside others such as you and Jessica.

"My wife Kim and I do not have a lot of money. I am paid well here, but with a young family, the best she and I can do is pay the bills and save a little as we go. Our families both emigrated from Korea and don't have money either, or so we thought. A couple months ago, Kim received word that her aunt in Korea passed away. The aunt had no children of her own, so she left her money to my wife and her sisters. It's not a huge amount. We could not run off and retire or anything. It is enough, though, to put something down for buying a piece of this company. I don't know a lot about the company's financial results, so I don't know enough to talk about price, but it seems pretty clear we are growing. I want to buy in now before we get so big that we cannot afford anything."

Jason stopped. That was the extent of his planned remarks. He and Kim wrote down questions that Robert may potentially ask and readied Jason's answers. They also discussed what Jason should do if Robert came right out and denied the request. The tactic now was to stop and see what Robert did next. Jason waited.

Robert unfolded his hands and uncrossed his legs, positioning himself closer to the table. Jason suspected his boss was gathering his thoughts.

"First of all, Jason, I am glad we are having this conversation. I admit that I am surprised by it, so I don't have any real specific response to give you."

Jason interrupted—perhaps too quickly, he later admitted during his debrief with Kim. "My intention was not to catch you off guard. I wanted to initially talk about this with you in person, as opposed to sending you an e-mail or something."

"That's fine, Jason. I don't have a response because we've never had an employee buy in before, so there's no precedent for this. Plus, I'd have to talk with Al before he and I could have any reaction."

"I assumed that you and Al would need to speak. I look forward to the chance to meet with you both. I approached you first, Robert, because I work for you. Also, I know you better than I know Al at this point."

"I would likely do the same in your situation. You are a fine performer here, and I want you here for the long-term. I am honored that you—and your wife, apparently—think highly enough of the company that you would consider buying into it."

"Thank you, Robert," Jason said, acknowledging the compliment. He hadn't heard a question, though, so he waited for the other man to continue.

"You said that you don't know much about our financial results. I presume that means you don't have a specific offer in mind?"

"No, I don't. We would need to know more before discussing specifics. I would need to meet with Reggie and get some financial information."

"One step at a time, Jason. Al and I need to meet next. I assure you that we will take this seriously. For now, I would appreciate it if you do not discuss this with anybody else, other than your wife, of course. Ownership is not a topic to discuss in the hallways or break room."

"Yes, sir."

"Can I ask you something before we wrap up? What would you have done without your wife's inheritance?"

Score another point for Kim. She guessed this question could come up. They knew mentioning the inheritance was important to demonstrate Jason's commitment, but they feared that Robert and Al might wrongly conclude that Jason's interest in ownership was created by the windfall. "I planned on having this conversation with you at some point, before we ever knew about my wife's inheritance. The money we received only means we could have this conversation with you sooner and offer to pay something upfront. I want to be a business owner, Robert. That's important to me and my family."

Jason saw his boss absorb this information. Later, Kim said it sounded like he handled it perfectly. Robert needed to know that Jason was serious about ownership, without having to come right out and say that without ownership he would leave Ark. There was no need for ultimatums. Robert knew Jason's value, and the risk and costs the company could incur if they lost him.

"Okay, Jason. Again, thank you for coming to me. I am honored. Give me some time to get with Al. I don't know how long, but likely it will take a week or two. There's a lot going on right now. I need you to please be patient, and keep up the good work until I can get back to you. Can you do that?"

"You bet, Robert. I'll wait. Thank you for meeting with me." Jason, as he and Kim agreed, stood first and extended his hand. Robert rose and took his hand, and nodded in dismissal.

On his way out of Robert's office, Jason looked at his watch. It read 7:37 a.m. Only seven minutes had passed, but for Jason it felt like an hour. He knew Kim would be waiting for his call, so he headed to the downstairs café to find a quiet place to call her away from office ears. Too excited to wait for an elevator, he took the stairs down, two steps at a time.

***

Robert watched Jason leave his office. The young man was a solid employee and an effective manager, smart and hardworking. And to Robert's surprise, Jason conducted himself that morning with more poise and leadership than Robert would have given him credit for prior to this meeting.

Robert quickly concluded he was open to sharing ownership with a quality employee like Jason. Jessica and Jason could be a good team one day, in much the same way he and Al had been all of these years. Jessica was certain to develop into the role of the outside person, the future face of the business. Jason could develop into the inside role, the person who ran day-to-day operations for the company. Given enough time and coaching, it was a potential winning team. Perhaps Jason could buy down a portion of Al's ownership. That might accomplish several positive outcomes at once.

The timing of Jason's inquiry was not ideal, however. Robert needed to sit down with Al and secure Jessica's future first. He would not consider some transaction with Jason without having a clear path for Jessica to have an ownership share, too. Yet Robert sensed that without ownership, Jason might leave the company. No employee is irreplaceable, but some are more expensive to lose than others. Losing Jason, with all of his customer contacts, could be costly. Robert was no stranger to such a dilemma.

Robert made a mental note to circle back with Jason in a few days and let him know again that he was appreciated. That would help keep the younger man engaged in addition to buying Robert some time. Then, Robert needed to meet with Al. The list of topics they had to discuss seemed to grow every day. Sitting at his desk chair, Robert opened up both his and Al's digital calendars. It was time to set up a meeting between the two of them.

Week 2

"Hey, are you ready?" Robert asked Al while standing in his office doorway.

"You bet," Al replied. He collected his notepad, sport coat, and car keys. "Let's go. I didn't know you were free for lunch today, Robert."

"At first I wasn't, but when I looked at both our calendars, this was perhaps our only chance over the next couple weeks to meet for any length of time. So I moved a couple things around to open up today."

The two men walked out of Ark's offices, stopping to chat with a few employees on the long walk from Al's office to the lobby. As they rode the elevator down and walked to Al's car, the co-owners mostly caught up on routine business matters and family. Never once did they discuss their destination. By tradition, their lunch meetings were always at a bustling, hole-in-the-wall barbeque shack down the street from their offices. The food was excellent, and the noise ironically allowed them to talk in relative privacy.

A few minutes later, Al carried his pulled pork platter over to an open table for two. Robert joined him with a barbecue chicken sandwich and chips. After they sat, both men created room on the small table for their organizational devices—Al, a notepad and Robert, an iPad.

"I am glad we are meeting," Al opened. "I have some things I would like to talk about, but you called this meeting, Robert, so you go first. Shoot."

"Thanks," Robert said, swallowing a bite of his sandwich. "I actually have several things for us to discuss. Let me start with Jason."

"Jason Lee? What's wrong?"

"Nothing, at least not yet. He wants to buy into Ark." Robert informed Al about the meeting with Jason last week and the young manager's request. Al listened patiently, asking a few clarifying questions along the way.

"I am surprised," Al reacted, "but in a good way. This is the first time we've ever had an employee offer to buy in, isn't it?"

"Yes. We've had a few employees over the years ask to be given ownership, but nothing serious. Jason did not ask for anything to be given to him. He said he is willing to buy in, and can make an offer once he knows more about the company's financial results. I have to tell you—he impressed me.

"Let me go ahead and say," Robert continued, "that I like Jason and want to keep him, but I would prefer to resolve a couple of things first before we consider his request. If we do this, it should be on our timetable, not Jason's. He is still somewhat new—"

"About a year, right?"

"Closer to eighteen months. If we are going to share ownership with anybody, I want to really know that person well before we do. We have been burned before."

"I completely agree. We should wait. He's doing a fine job for us, but I hardly know the young man."

Robert suspected Al would latch onto the idea that they needed to get to know Jason better. Robert worked closely with Jason, but Al did not. "We can't just do nothing, though, Al. I sensed pretty strongly that Jason will leave us if we tell him the door is permanently closed."

Al shook his head. "I don't want to lose him either. Perhaps the three of us should meet and tell him that he has a bright future with us, but we need more time. Over lunch. That will give me an opportunity to get to know him better."

"That sounds good to me. I will set up the lunch. It may take several weeks to find a time for all three of us, given how busy we are right now. But, Al, please make a point of telling him that you know about his inquiry, and you are pleased to discuss it with him. Let him know we are treating him seriously."

Al nodded and made a note on his pad.

Both men were pleased with the strategy to stall their employee's request, although they each possessed different motives.

"What's next on your list, Robert?"

"Can we talk about the issue of changing commissions for the sales team on project work?"

"Yes, that topic is on my list of things to discuss, too. But . . . hmm . . . would you mind if I talked about something first? I want to put this issue in some greater context, as I wasn't able to do so with Dan in the room when this issue first came up."

Robert felt unsure about where Al was going, but he shrugged his shoulders in acquiescence and took a large bite of his sandwich.

"Do you remember about a month ago when I went to the IT industry association conference in DC? Well, while there I had dinner with a guy I know from the association. He sold his business last year for a great price. During dinner, he spent two hours walking me through his company sale and how the process worked. He also took me through what made his IT company more valuable at sale. One of the key issues was the mix of revenue. According to him, buyers prefer businesses with ongoing, recurring revenues rather than project-based revenues, because projects are one-and-done. It makes sense. I'd feel that way if we were buying a company.

"Well," Al continued, not missing a beat, "that got me thinking about our business. We are enjoying a lot of growth, Robert, most of it because of the hard work you and I have put into this company. Over the last few years, an increasing amount of our revenue is coming from these projects. It is good work, and we're making some money from it. But all of this project work might not be making our business more valuable. If project work becomes too large a piece of our total revenue, it could actually make our business less valuable to buyers."

"Wait," Robert said slowly, "you had this conversation a month ago? I don't get it, Al. Why are we talking about this now?"

"I know, that is my fault. If you remember, I mentioned to you when I came back that I wanted to tell you about the trip, especially my dinner with this guy. We had a meeting set up a week or so after my return, but you had to cancel our lunch due to some customer issue. I am not blaming you," Al quickly explained. "I should have found another time for us to meet. But we've all been so busy lately. It just got away from me." Al paused to have a bite of his lunch, and to discern Robert's mood before proceeding.

"All right, it's no big deal, Al. I think I can see where this is going. You want us to cut our sales commissions on project work because you are worried the project work is growing into too big of the pie, right? I'm not sure I fully agree with you, but even if I did, so what? I mean, why care about how much project work we do if we are making a lot of money doing it?"

"It's a little different from that. I am worried that our focus on project work is slowing the growth of our core business, the ongoing service contracts. Have you seen our sales funnel report? For quite some time, project work has dominated the proposal list. We are selling more new projects than we are selling new service contracts. That is the part that has me concerned. If both sides of our business were growing at the same rate, that might be different.

"Plus, I am not sure we are making as much money from projects as you might think."

"Yeah, Reggie said something to me about that," Robert replied warily. "I am not sure why you and Reggie were discussing this without me."

"Reggie and I didn't discuss anything," Al said to placate his partner. "I asked him to model the financial changes if we were to cut the commission rate on project work. I also wanted to know how profitable each type of work was for us, so that we could have this very conversation. Reggie said he could not model profitability by type of work because we don't accurately allocate our costs to each type of work. Take, for example, your salary and mine. That's overhead. To accurately know how profitable project work and service work are for us, we would need to assign the appropriate portion of our salaries to each type of work."

"Reggie is making this too complicated, Al. That's easy—just assign us fifty-fifty. Assign half of our salary to each type of work. Heck, we should go ahead and allocate all of our costs fifty-fifty."

"That's not realistic, Robert," Al replied. "We have many expenses which more directly support one type of work rather than the other. Take you, for example. Over the last year or two, you probably have spent seventy-five percent of your time focused on project work for us. If we wanted to accurately know how profitable our project work is for us, we'd need to allocate seventy-five percent of your salary to project work. We don't do that today."

"Are you accusing me of spending too much time doing project work?"

"That's not necessarily what I am saying—"

"Not necessarily? Al, have you seen the increases to our bottom line the last few years? What are you complaining about?"

"Calm down, Robert. I am not complaining. Yes, I have seen the top- and bottom-line growth we have created. What I am trying to point out is that we walk around talking about how profitable our project work is, because it brings in large lump sums of cash. But cash and profits are two different things. We need to accurately model our costs in order to know how profitable the project work really is. Without doing that, we are just guessing."

"Fine, Al," Robert acquiesced, eyebrows furrowed. "If you want Reggie to accurately assign costs, that's okay with me. I still don't understand why you asked him to model cutting commissions on project work. Like you just said, it's anybody's guess at this point how profitable our project work really is. Why do you want us to sell less project work? You and I both know that salespeople will sell what we pay them to sell. Cutting commissions there is the same thing as telling everybody to sell less of it."

"That goes back to my meeting with this guy in DC. Even if we are making money doing project work, it may not be increasing our company's value."

"Again, Al, I've got to ask, so what? We are making money. We have had several record years in a row. Who cares if it makes us less valuable in somebody else's eyes? It's not like we are selling this thing anytime soon." Robert chuckled, pouring hot sauce from a plastic bottle onto his sandwich and taking another bite.

Al said nothing. Robert stopped chewing and stared at his partner as if a total stranger had just sat at the lunch table. He forcibly swallowed the food in his mouth.

"You want to sell? Now? When we're making all this money? Why, for heaven's sake? When were you going to tell me? Don't I have any say in this?"

"Of course I want to sell. What did you think, that I would die at my desk one day?" Al checked himself. He rehearsed this part of the conversation several times, but already his frustration was building.

"No, I never thought you wanted to work until you drop dead. I don't either. But why now? You're a young guy, and so am I. We are making a ton of money right now, and the next few years look even brighter—"

"That's exactly why we should sell now. We are very profitable. That drives up our value—well, potentially it does, depending on our revenue mix. The future does look strong. That increases our potential value as well. You don't sell when you are in decline, Robert. You sell when you are on a strong upswing. And thank you, Robert, I am glad you think that I am a younger guy—but I'm not. I am sixty-two. I want to sell at some point when Valerie and I have lots of good years left, God willing, to do the things that we denied ourselves up to this point. We sacrificed a lot for our kids and for this business. I don't want to sell when I am too old and frail to enjoy myself."

Robert sat listening, hands on the table. Thoughts of his food were all forgotten. "When were you going to tell me all of this, Al?"

"I am telling you now. That's why we are talking. It's not like I want to sell next Thursday or anything. We have time to plan this out, and do things our way."

"You may be telling me now, but it sounds like you made up your mind some time ago."

"No, that's not the case. No lightbulb suddenly went off over my head. I have been thinking about this for a few months and talking about it with Valerie. I told Linda Hamill last week that I felt this way. Otherwise, you are the first to know."

Al could see Robert was taken aback. He needed to steer the conversation back to a positive direction.

"Robert, this is not just about me. It's about you too. We both made sacrifices for this business. You certainly shared in the risks as well. I know how big Ricardo's company was—Ricardo was the guy in DC—and what he sold for. I think we could get a similar price. It would be a lot of money, Robert. Selling Ark will be great for you and your family. You are even younger than me, and that gives you even more time to enjoy with Tess and your kids. You could keep on working after a sale, if you prefer. Anybody would take you. Or, set up a brand-new business of your own. You will have all these options."

Robert sat silently, rolling the hot-sauce dispenser back and forth in his hand.

"What are you thinking, Robert? I know this is not something we've talked about until now. But like you said, neither one of us wants to work here forever. This day was going to come someday. I am only suggesting that someday is coming soon."

Robert could hear Al's enthusiasm. He recognized the good points Al made. Yes, it made sense to sell the business when their profits were strongest. And yes, Al and Valerie should be able to travel and do whatever they wanted to do while they were still young enough to do it. Yet there was still something wrong.

In that moment, Robert realized that he resented Al for reaching this decision without talking to him. Al never asked him what he wanted. Now, if he shared his ideas about keeping Ark for another ten years while preparing Jessica to take over, he would be throwing a large wrench directly into Al's plans. Robert did not want to spoil things for Al or his family. He cared for the man. Yet Robert's competing vision for their future would now be the Johnny-come-lately whenever he finally did bring it up. Right then, Robert decided that if Al was not going to ask him for his input on a topic as important as this, then he was not going to offer it.

"Al, I am just floored . . . that's all. It's a lot to take in. Needless to say, I did not know this was on your agenda for our lunch today."

Al listened for any objection from Robert. Hearing none, he interpreted that to mean his co-owner was on board to proceed. "I realize it's a lot to take in, Robert. Again, I am sorry we did not talk about my DC meeting before. All of us have just been so busy."

Al paused again, waiting to see if Robert was going to say anything more. Robert did not.

"Look, partner, we will take this slowly. You and I have never sold a business before, so we probably have a bit to learn. We are in the best possible spot in that we don't *have* to sell, so we can control things and do it the right way. We have employees and customers who are important to us, and we will want to make sure this is a good thing for them too.

"I got a referral from Wilson Riley to an investment banker here in Atlanta who apparently works with IT companies. I spoke to him, and he's agreed to give us an estimated sale price for the business. He also will answer all of our questions about how this process works, and what we would need to do to get ready."

"How is he going to tell us what our business is worth? He doesn't know anything about—wait a minute. Did you already meet with him?"

"No, Robert, I did not. I only spoke to him once on the phone. He provided me with a nondisclosure agreement, an NDA, and then I sent him our financial statements. He's agreed to meet with us next week if we want. That's all."

"That's all? That sounds like a lot."

"It's just gathering information. He's not charging us anything. It's his job to keep this confidential. We have nothing to lose by learning what the company might be worth."

Robert shrugged his shoulders. "All right, I guess."

"Thanks. I will set up the meeting for next week. This will be great, Robert. You'll see."

Robert watched Al as they finished lunch. His partner did most of the talking, smiling and laughing, in one of the best moods Robert could remember Al enjoying in a long time. Robert, however, struggled to eat, as his food suddenly tasted flat. During the short drive back to the office, Robert stared out the side window as Al told him about his upcoming summer vacation to Tuscany.

***

Later that afternoon, Al sat at his desk catching up on e-mails. One he noticed came from Linda Hamill. It read:

To:	*Al Beaman, James Rigney*
From:	*Linda C.*
Message:	*Al and James—I want to connect you two.*

Al and James,

Al, after our one-on-one meeting last week, I thought James could be a resource for you. I encourage you to meet with him. His website says that he and his firm "help business owners plan for and achieve successful exits." I specifically thought of James after our conversation about you and Robert, Al. Perhaps James can help you guys figure some things out together.

James, Al is a successful CEO and owner of an IT services company, and a member of one of my CEO groups. He and his partner are thinking about their exit plans. Perhaps you could be of help to them.

I copied and pasted each of your contact info below. I will leave it up to you two to connect.

Cheers!

Linda C.

Al reread the e-mail one more time before hitting the Reply All button. He typed:

To:	*Linda C., James Rigney*
From:	*Al Beaman*
Message:	*Thank you*

Linda and James,

Thank you Linda, for the connection. I appreciate you following up with me. However, it may be unnecessary. My partner Robert and I are working with an investment banker who came well recommended, and we seem to be moving forward.

James, if we need anything I'll contact you. Thanks.

Al

Al deleted Linda's message and moved on to the rest of his pending e-mails. About fifteen minutes later, just when he thought he had cleared his inbox, a new message alert flashed on his screen. Al scrolled up to see a reply to his previous message to Linda and James Rigney. The reply came from James. It read:

To:	*Linda C., Al Beaman*
From:	*James Rigney*
Message:	*Thanks for the connection*

Linda, thanks for the connection. Al, good to meet you, at least online. If you and your partner are planning on selling within the next few months, then I agree that you likely don't need an exit planner. There's not any time left to do anything. In that case, you need a good investment banker. It sounds like you may have one.

If you and your partner get stuck along the way, or if it looks like it may take more time than you thought to get ready for sale, I am glad to discuss things with you.

Otherwise, good luck!

James

Al deleted the message.

Week 3

Thursday, 1:35 p.m., in the conference room
at Peachtree Capital Market Partners, Buckhead

"So, that's what our company is worth?" Al asked, jumping to the bottom line of the report.

"It's our estimate of the price range you could see if you took your business to market at this time. Ultimately, what any business is worth is only determined by what a willing buyer will pay a willing seller." Taylor Collins, of Peachtree Capital Market Partners, knew from thirty years' investment banking experience the importance of using precise language when discussing with business owners what their company might be worth.

Robert rapidly flipped back and forth between various tables and bar charts in Taylor's report. "Would you please explain again how you came up with this value range? I want to make sure I understand how this works."

To appease Al, Robert reluctantly agreed to let the investment banker do this analysis for them. Robert, however, did not want to sell his interest in the business. He wanted to continue working for at least another ten years, and then pass his interest in the business to his daughter Jessica. Yet he could not deny that Al did have something of a point when he said that there was no harm in learning what the company could be worth. Also, Robert had to admit that if the number was so high that he would never have to work again, that might get his attention. Jessica was talented enough to land on her feet if the company was sold. However, the number would have to be a very surprising, very high number.

"Sure," Taylor replied to Robert. "There are a variety of ways to estimate the value of a closely held business. Here, we are using the market approach, which means we estimate the value range based on the sale of comparable companies in the market. It's similar to, at least in this one way, pricing a home for sale. Before listing your home, you likely ask the real estate agent to pull a list of comparable home listings and sales, called 'comps,' to determine the market value of your home at that point in time. Comparable homes are those that have similar location, size, amenities, and construction quality. When referring to a business, comparable transactions are those within the same industry, business model, and size range, with sometimes geographic location playing a factor.

"In our report, we identified nearly two dozen comparable transactions. Your industry has quite a bit of sale activity right now. That gives us a good data set to reference. Based on these comps, we estimate that the company could sell for somewhere in the price range that you see summarized here at the bottom." Taylor paused to make sure the two owners followed his explanation. He also was waiting for the next question, which he felt certain was coming.

"How come some companies sell for the high end of this range, and some sell for the lower end?" Al asked, fulfilling Taylor's prediction. "The difference is pretty significant. Is it just due to company size?"

"Size does matter," Taylor answered. "Bigger companies in the same industry generally sell for a higher multiple of their earnings than smaller companies."

"What do you mean by 'multiple of earnings'?" Robert interrupted impatiently.

Taylor silently chided himself. "Sorry, I should have explained that. 'Multiple of earnings' is a way to express the company's sale price as some number multiplied by its pre-tax earnings. So if a hypothetical company had pre-tax earnings of two million dollars and sold for ten million, then we would say the multiple of earning was five."

Taylor waited for another question. Hearing none, he moved on. "A widget manufacturer with ten million dollars in pre-tax profits likely sells for a higher multiple of earnings than a widget manufacturer doing one million dollars in pre-tax profits, all other factors held aside. When pulling market comps, we don't want bigger companies to inflate the average, so we either exclude them from the sample set, or discount their multiples to bring them in line with companies of your size. So the answer to your question is yes, size does matter. But, in this analysis prepared for you, the transactions were all reasonably similar in size to Ark."

"If the differences between the high and low prices were not about size," Robert asked, "why did some of these companies sell for a higher multiple and others sell for a lower multiple? You would think companies of similar size would all sell for similar multiples."

"That's another important question, Robert." The investment banker made a show of closing his copy of the report and pushing it a few inches away. "How much your business does in revenue and profits is where buyers start. From there, they want to know how your business achieved those results. They look at a range of issues within your company which may make it more or less valuable to them."

Al remembered his conversation with Ricardo Reed and recognized where Taylor was going. "You are referring to things like how dependent the business is on its owners and how diversified our customer base is, right?"

"Exactly," Taylor replied. "Those are two of many important issues that present either opportunity or risk to a buyer. Taking those examples in reverse, buyers understandably see risk if one or a few customers account for a large portion of revenues and profits. If that is true, many buyers will reduce the price they are willing to pay for that business. As for the issue of owner dependency, a business that can't function without its owners is also a less valuable business to many buyers. Relatedly, buyers are often attracted to companies with high-performing employees, especially management teams. It's also important in most cases that those employees have signed noncompete and nonsolicitation agreements."

Al and Robert shared a look. Taylor noticed.

"You don't have noncompete or nonsolicitation agreements in place for your employees?" Taylor asked, reopening the report to take a few notes.

"No, we don't," Al explained. "We used to have them many years ago, but we stopped as we grew. For a while we were growing so fast that we lost track of some things. Later, we talked about it and decided against requiring them. We have a family atmosphere at Ark. Our culture is important to us, and we trust our people. Plus, we know from a past incident that those agreements are all but impossible to enforce."

Taylor addressed Al. "I am not an attorney, so I cannot speak directly to the legal enforceability. However, noncompete and nonsolicitation agreements are not worthless, even if difficult to enforce. Buyers appreciate their deterrence effect. Some employees actually are good people who will, upon separation from employment, respect the agreement that they signed. Other employees may have ideas about taking customers or coworkers with them upon separation, but the threat of a legal fight stays their hand.

"But I do get what you're saying about your company's culture, Al. Many successful business owners rightly pride themselves on having a warm, trusting culture. Buyers may like your culture, too. But keep in mind that they won't know your employees. Buying a company brings change, and change is unpredictable. Anything that reduces a buyer's risk, such as noncompete and nonsolicitation employee agreements, potentially increases sale value."

"Well, Taylor, that does make sense," Al acknowledged, writing now in his own report copy. "We might have made a mistake with that one."

"Don't beat yourself up. It is a common mistake. You can have a family-oriented culture but still adopt practices that protect the business. Either way, you should address that issue before attempting to sell your business." Taylor paused while Al finished taking some notes.

Looking up from his writing, Al posed another question. "Can you talk about revenue mix? We have been discussing that internally. Does it make a difference to buyers if our revenue comes from service contracts or project work?"

"Can you give me a little bit more on this?" Taylor requested. "Are the service contracts longer term? What does a typical project look like? Do project customers ever hire you for repeat projects?"

"Our service contracts tend to be longer term," Al explained. "While the contracts themselves are annually renewable, the average service customer stays with us more than seven years. As for the projects, there is a wide variety. We design and install new IT systems, consult on client-relationship management software, and do some training work. Most projects last only a few weeks or months. Rarely does a customer hire us for more than one project."

Robert jumped in, suspicious that Al was trying to maneuver the discussion. "That's not quite the case. Some customers have hired us for more than one project. We are working on a large customer right now who has a second big project for us. Also, don't overlook the fact that we cross-sell our project customers and go after the IT service work once the project is over."

Taylor sensed that the two business owners were competing against each other on this issue, and was unsure why. "I didn't know that your revenue was a mix of service engagements and project work. It was not clearly broken out in your income statement, from what I saw."

"We don't really code the revenue by type in our accounting systems," Al said. "But, we know which customers are service customers, and which customers are project customers. We could go back and make the changes so that the breakout shows up on the income statement."

"That would work in some cases, Al," Robert interjected. "But many customers use us for both types of work. With those customers, the two types of revenue will be lumped together."

"Yes, Robert, but we really don't have that many customers who use us for both types of work."

"It happens more often than you might be aware of," Robert replied, doing his best to keep his rising frustration in check. "It will increase in the future, too."

"What will increase?" Taylor asked.

"Robert believes our cross-selling results will increase in the future," Al answered for his partner. "He believes more customers will be both service and project customers."

"I know they will, Al. You'd know too if you were more involved with customers."

Turning to face Taylor, Al made a visible effort to maintain his composure. "Yes, well, what is undeniably true is that project work is an increasingly greater portion of our total revenue—"

"And profits too—our revenue *and* our profits," Robert interrupted.

Al paused to let the interruption pass, then resumed speaking to Taylor. "My question is, does the mix of our revenue—how much comes from service work and project work—matter to potential buyers? If it does matter, then how?"

In his career, Taylor had sold several hundred businesses, many of which had multiple owners. It was clear that Al and Robert disagreed on where their business was today, and where each wanted to take it. After a brief moment, he addressed both of them. "Guys, several things jump out at me from this short discussion. First, if you two are not completely sure what your numbers look like, then a buyer won't know either. By numbers, I am not referring just to your revenue and profits, but also to your revenue mix, cross-selling results, profitability by revenue type, and so on. I like a healthy debate as much as the next guy, but when it's time to sell your business, you cannot be unsure about where your revenue comes from and how you get it."

Taylor let that sink in for a moment before continuing. "To answer Al's question, revenue mix matters. Service work is recurring in nature, and buyers like recurring revenue. Robert, I appreciate that some of the customers do repeat project work and some convert into service contracts—the actual amounts to be determined—but project work is nonrecurring in nature. In many situations, buyers pay less for nonrecurring revenue because it happens infrequently and may be less predictable."

"So if our project work is increasing at the expense of our service work, this could make our company less valuable to a buyer?" Al put the question directly to Taylor.

"Yes, that could occur," Taylor acknowledged.

Al felt vindicated. He hoped Robert would finally listen to him.

Taylor continued, "For that reason, you need to clearly distinguish between service and project work in your financial statements before trying to sell your business."

"We will make that change, Taylor," Al volunteered. "I think we can get that done rather easily."

Taylor waited for Robert to disagree or dispute Al's optimism, but the other owner remained silent. Taylor therefore returned to an earlier topic. "One of you mentioned earlier that you have written contracts with your customers. Is that correct?"

"Yes," Al replied, "we typically have signed agreements in place with both our project and service customers."

"Are the contracts yours or your customers? Meaning, do you provide the contract, or does your customer?"

Al waited for Robert, but his partner made no effort to answer, so he continued. "Both. Some customers, usually the larger ones, require us to use a contract they provide. Our smaller customers typically use our contract."

"Got it. Have you reviewed the contracts to see if they have any provisions that prohibit or restrict assignment of the contract, such as upon sale of your business?"

Al and Robert looked at each other, clearly stumped by the question. Al answered. "No, but I'm not clear on what you mean."

Taylor put his pen down again and folded his hands on the conference room table, an unconscious habit when he explained something to prospects or clients. "Generally speaking, contracts are freely assignable unless a statute, or the contract itself, prevents assignment. In light of this, many businesses put an anti-assignment clause in their contract, which prohibits assignment without their consent. The contract which you provide customers probably does not contain such a clause. However, customers large enough to require you to use their contract often insert anti-assignment clauses. Sometimes those clauses specifi-cally prohibit assignment upon sale of the business, without the customer's written approval.

"Here's why this is important. Many business sales are structured as asset sales, which means the buyer does not buy your *company*, but rather buys only the assets it wants within your company, such as the accounts receivable, physical property, customer contracts, and so on. In an asset sale, a contract that contains an anti-assignment provision will require getting the customer's consent to continue doing business with that customer post-sale. That takes time and work, and creates risk."

"Risk that a customer might say no?" Robert asked to confirm Taylor's point.

"Yes, clearly one risk is the customer might go away. There's another risk, however. The customer will know that a sale is occurring, and that the seller and buyer are eager to protect it. A shrewd customer likely uses the sale to negotiate more favorable pricing or terms. That would reduce business profits going forward."

Taylor waited to make sure he had Al and Robert's full attention before continuing. "Gentlemen, my firm would like to represent your company for sale when it's ready. From the preliminary numbers you gave me, you're profitable and growing. Ark has a solid reputation in the market. Furthermore, there is a lot of activity in your industry right now. Our firm already knows several strategic buyers and private equity groups who could be interested. That's the good news."

That last phrase had the desired impact. The two business owners noticeably leaned forward to listen as Taylor continued.

"Here's the bad news. If I were in your situation, I would address the issues we discussed today before starting the process to sell. You have to differentiate between service revenue and project revenue in your financial statements. I would also recommend getting the company's financials audited by your accountants. If you have never been audited before, the process may uncover additional issues to address prior to sale.

"Beyond that, I recommend you implement employee agreements which contain noncompete, nonsolicitation, and nondisclosure provisions. Next, you absolutely need to review your customer contracts and identify any that contain anti-assignment language.

"We uncovered this handful of items after just one meeting together. If we continued to discuss your company, we could uncover additional areas for improvement prior to sale. Please don't hear all gloom and doom in this. You built a solid business, and that's the hard part. But growing a business and preparing a business for sale are two different things. The issues we've talked about today are common among small to midsized businesses. You both have a lot to gain by addressing these needs prior to pursuing a sale, including potentially a higher sale price, better terms, and a quicker and less stressful process."

Taylor watched as the two business owners absorbed all of his offered information. Both sat silently, making an obvious effort to avoid eye contact with each other. Finally, Al asked a question. "How long would all of this take, in your experience?"

"I would say six to twelve months at a minimum."

Al could not contain his disbelief. "What? Why so long? To get an audit and review our customer contracts should only take a few weeks, maybe a month or two at best."

Taylor shook his head in disagreement. "If you two left this office and made getting ready for sale your absolute highest priority, and had the help of an experienced management team and quality advisors, then maybe it could take a few months to address the issues we discussed today. But, that assumes you don't get any nasty surprises or uncover any additional issues. Unfortunately, you likely will. Plus, you will have less time than you think to work on these issues because you cannot take your foot off the gas pedal at your company. It is critically important that you keep the business growing and profitable. Buyers place high value on a positive trend, and will often walk away from a potential sale if the business's performance starts to slip."

"Okay, let's assume you are correct, Taylor," Al conceded after a moment. "Once we address these issues, and assuming there are no nasty surprises, then how long to sell the company once you get started?"

"Once we are formally engaged, it typically takes six to nine months to run the process. It can take less or more time, of course, but most companies take about that long."

"After the sale," Al asked, "would Robert and I be free to do other things?"

"We have not even talked about that issue today. I don't know enough at this point about your business to answer the question. If either of you play an important role in the business's sales or operations, a buyer may require you to stick around after the sale. Guys, don't take this the wrong way, but Robert, you are younger and therefore a buyer may naturally focus on keeping you involved after the sale for a longer period of time. Ultimately it comes down to your role in the company today, how replaceable you are, and your own desire to work or not after the sale." Taylor suspected he was opening a can of worms with his answer to that question. He also suspected it was not the first can opened during this meeting.

Taylor waited to see if Al and Robert had any more questions for him. After neither owner spoke, he continued.

"Let's do this. Let's start with breaking out your service revenue versus project revenue on your income statement, and see where that leaves us. Al, you said you would champion that. Work with your team and get me the corrected income statements as soon as possible. Once I have them, then let's talk about what the picture looks like."

"Got it," Al agreed. "Thanks for all your help, Taylor. We'll do that. And thank you for this report, too. We would be excited to sell the company for a price in the range you gave us. We appreciate your time and advice. I'll get you those updated income statements right away."

Al stood up and enthusiastically shook Taylor's hand, thanking him again. Robert stood and shook hands with Taylor as well, but only offered a quick nod of his head to the investment banker.

As they walked out of the office suite, Al turned to Robert. "Hey, I know we took separate cars over here, but maybe we can get a cup of coffee downstairs and talk for a few minutes about what we just heard?"

"Sorry, Al, I can't. I have another appointment. This meeting ran longer than I had planned, so I will need to rush. I've got a few calls to make along the way as well. We'll catch up later."

Al watched Robert walk away. He sensed Robert had some reservations about selling the company, but it was normal to have a little case of the jitters. Robert also probably had some understandable concerns about Jessica. But Taylor's market estimates had looked strong. Both of them should jump at the chance to sell the business for a price within the range the investment banker presented. Preparing the company for sale apparently would take a little longer than anticipated, but Al was willing the do the extra work while Robert focused on day-to-day operations. Al was confident Robert would eventually get excited. There was a lot of money at stake, money both men had earned.

Al knew Robert often needed time to process important or complex business decisions. He would give his partner a few days, and then circle back to discuss their next steps. Maybe this person Taylor mentioned could help them get the business ready for sale faster. Perhaps the person could help Al talk some sense into Robert, if it came down to that, although Al doubted it would. Robert was a good man.

***

Five minutes later, Robert sat in his car holding open the report from Taylor Collins. Robert circled the estimated price range for their company. The numbers were good, maybe even higher than he expected. He felt blessed to own half of a business potentially worth this amount of money.

He lay the report on the open passenger seat next to him and started the car. As he pulled out of the lot, Robert called Shannon Stewart on his speaker phone. A short conversation with her confirmed his fears. Even if they sold the business for the high end of the report's range, Robert would be unable to retire. His half of the sale proceeds, minus taxes, would be too little. He was too young, and he still had three children not yet in college. He would have to continue working.

Working was not the problem for Robert. He loved his job. The problem was if they sold the company, Robert would likely find himself reporting to some new, as yet unknown boss. He had no desire to go down that road. After seventeen years working for himself alongside Al, why should he put himself in that position? Even if they sold the company and the new owner released Robert after a short stay, by then he would be in his midfifties and either needing a job or facing the daunting task of starting up a new business. Those options were even less appealing.

Then there was Jessica. A sale of Ark denied Jessica the chance to succeed him within his own company. He knew that she could find a new career path if he sold the business, but why should he deny her that opportunity when he did not have to? All of this because Al apparently wanted to hit the beach sooner rather than later.

Robert could not deny the sense of betrayal he felt by Al's selfishness. Sure, Al had a right to retire if that's what he wanted. But Al's retirement should not derail all of Robert's personal and family goals. That was not right either.

The way Robert saw it, Al had not fully considered the possibility of winding down his own involvement in the business over the next five to ten years. Robert was sure Al could be happy slowly shedding his responsibilities, reducing his stress and taking more and longer vacations each year. Al already wasn't working as hard as he once did, Robert noted with a touch of resentment. Maybe he and Jessica could buy some of Al's ownership along the way. That would get Al additional cash while he still collected a paycheck. This was a better plan. He would present it to Al, once Al was ready, and once Al asked him. After two decades working together, he knew Al got easily excited by the latest great idea, but eventually came back down to planet earth. In the meantime, their company was growing, and Robert needed to get back on track implementing his ideas on how to create even more growth. Al would see that they'd be crazy to sell their business now, when the future was so bright.

Robert felt a little better as he merged onto the highway. He did have another appointment to get to, but the meeting with Taylor had wrapped up earlier than he expected, so he was not in a rush.

Friday, 8:10 a.m.,
in the employee break room at Ark Technology Solutions Inc.

"Good morning, Reggie. I'm glad I bumped into you," Robert smiled. "Remember that cash-flow forecast you were going to do tied to potentially hiring a project manager? You can skip it. We don't need it anymore."

"Oh? We are not doing that now?" Reggie asked, looking up from his breakfast. "You two guys must have talked about it. Good. That's real good."

"Please get with Teri in HR and make sure they have finalized the draft job description and comp package. I intend to start interviewing for the position right away," Robert said.

"Wait—huh? I thought you just said we were not going to hire a PM."

"I didn't say that. I said we don't need the cash-flow forecast. I intend to hire a PM as soon as possible."

"But you wanted to know if we could make the hire without cutting into our cash reserves. Without that forecast, I don't know how much this reduces our cash going forward."

"We have plenty of cash, Reggie. It's okay if we dip into some of it. This is an important move for us. Please huddle up with HR and make sure we are ready for when I find somebody. Thanks." Robert walked out.

Reggie watched Robert's back as his boss left the break room. Had Al and Robert discussed this? Where did that leave the issue of cutting commissions on project work? Reggie felt unsure. What he was sure of was that he was behind in their month-end financial close. He'd get with Teri and make sure she was ready for Robert's new hire. Reggie popped his last piece of bacon into his mouth, threw away the paper plate, and made for his office. The day was a-marchin' on, as his mother used to say.

Later that same morning,
Al's office at Ark Technology Solutions Inc.

"Dan, thanks for coming in. I want to proceed with the commission reduction on project-related work that we have been discussing. Please give me by next week your ideas on how you want to implement this within your sales team."

"I will, Al." Dan Alvarez paused for a moment. "Does this mean that you are okay with whatever numbers Reggie came up with? I never heard one way or another."

"We never got that far. After thinking further about this, it's just a reduced payout when your team sells a project engagement. The lower payout simply results in a higher gross profit on that engagement. I don't think there is much there for Reggie to model."

"And you understand that our project-related sales could slow down with this change?"

"We are an IT services firm—not a project firm. We need to get back to growing our core service offering. Besides, it's not like your salespeople will just go hungry, Dan. They will go back to selling service contracts."

The sound of an unanswered phone ringing somewhere down the hall drifted into Al's office.

"Okay, Al. I'll have the implementation steps written up by next week for you to review."

In response, Al spun his desk chair around to directly face his desktop computer screen. Dan took that as his dismissal, and left the office to return to the day's activities.

Week 4

"Pssst . . . Dad, do you have a minute?"

"Sure, Jessica." Robert pulled the office phone receiver away from his ear. "I'm on hold. What's up?"

"Why are we cutting commissions on project work sales?"

"Huh? We aren't. Where did you hear this?"

"From Dan."

"When?"

"About fifteen minutes ago."

Robert slammed the phone receiver into its cradle. "What are you talking about?"

Jessica, surprised by her father's reaction, tentatively walked to his desk and sat in one of the arm chairs. "Dan and I were going over my quarterly sales goals. Then he told me that commission rates would be reduced on sales for project work. He said he and Al were working on the final numbers, so he didn't have any specifics to give me. He said he wanted to give me advanced notice because so much of my sales are project-related. He said that there would be a transition plan so that none of the salespeople take a compensation hit in the short term. But Dad, I sell a lot of project work—maybe more than anyone else. A commission reduction is going to hurt me. What's going on?"

Robert picked up a pen and gripped it tightly under his desk. He did not want his daughter to see his hands shaking.

"I'll get with Dan—and Al. Don't worry about this, honey," Robert said, unconsciously switching to how he addressed her outside of work.

"There was some talk about this, but we had not decided anything. I was completely against it. Let me find out what's going on."

"Okay, I guess. Please let me know what you find out."

As Robert stood up, Jessica followed. He walked her out of his office, all the while resisting a father's desire to give her a hug before she left. Robert counted to thirty to make sure his daughter was well out of sight, then walked down the hall to Dan Alvarez's office.

***

Dan Alvarez was less than five minutes into a meeting with his marketing support team when there came a knock at his office door. Before he could reply, the door opened to reveal Robert Gilmore.

"Dan, can I have a minute?"

"Sure, Robert," Dan replied, masking his irritation for the interruption. "Can I get back to you in a bit? We just started this meeting."

"No. It's important." Dan could see a hard, stern look on the other man's face. Whatever it was, Robert was not going to be put off.

"Check," he said to Robert. He stood and made his way to the door, saying to his team, "Please review those new materials without me. I'll be back in a minute."

Robert stepped back from the doorway, giving Dan room to join him in the hallway. Dan closed his office door behind him, thinking of a tactful way to ask Robert to not barge into his office. Yet before he could say anything, Robert stepped forward, getting uncomfortably close.

"What's the deal with the commission reduction on project work, Dan?"

"What? What about it?" Dan involuntarily took a half step back, only to feel the heel of his foot hit the closed door behind him.

"'What about it?' Who said you could make that change? I never approved it."

Robert was seething. Focused on maintaining his own composure, Dan took a small step to the side, restoring a little space between them. He also quickly looked up and down the hallway to confirm that they were alone.

"Look, Robert, you were in the room when we discussed this. I could tell you were not in support of it at that time, but—"

"Then why did you think you could change it?"

"Because Al told me to. With all due respect, Robert, Al is the CEO and my boss. I'm vice president of sales, and I report to him. He told me we were proceeding with this change. I never thought of you." Dan instantly realized that this was the wrong thing to say. "What I mean is, I just assumed you and Al talked about this."

"He is the CEO and half owner. I own the other half. Reducing our project work going forward impacts our revenue and profits, and therefore I have a say in whether we do this or not. And I say 'no.'"

Dan heard voices and light laughter to his left. Reggie Chase and several other employees were walking toward them from down the hallway. Dan needed to diffuse this confrontation before it went any further.

"Robert, look, I will—"

"No, you look, Dan." Robert pointed a finger directly at him. "You will immediately stop telling our staff that we are cutting commissions. I will find Al. You will do nothing until you hear from him *and* me. Is that clear?"

Reggie and the small crowd were still walking toward them, but must have sensed something was wrong as the group was no longer talking amongst themselves, but rather watching Dan and Robert.

"Check. Robert, I will do nothing until I hear back from you and Al." Dan held his hands open, palms forward, indicating assent. There was nothing in Robert's demands that conflicted with Al's instructions to him.

Robert blinked hard, reminding Dan of a computer rebooting. He took a step back and, seemingly for the first time, noticed Reggie and the other employees only a few office doors away and advancing. He turned and walked away. Dan watched him leave.

Half a moment later, Reggie and the other employees arrived. Reggie made a motion for the others in his group to continue without him. They leaned and squeezed to get around their colossal colleague in the narrow office hallway.

Once the two of them were alone, Reggie looked down at Dan and asked, "What was that about?"

"That, good buddy," Dan answered, "is what happens when two business owners are not talking to one another."

"Oh. So we are not hiring a project manager."

"What?" Dan felt confused for the second time in as many minutes. "No. That delightful little chat was about cutting commissions on project-related sales. What project manager? What are you talking about, Reggie?"

Reggie reached down to put one of his catcher's-mitt-sized hands on Dan's shoulder. "You don't know about our new project manager? It sounds like we need to talk, 'good buddy.'"

"Yes, it does. I am right in the middle of a marketing meeting." Reggie looked around at the empty hallway. "Well, I am supposed to be in the middle of a meeting. It's going on without me, in my own office, right now. Let me catch up with you later, okay?"

Reggie gave him a salute and continued down the hallway. Dan took a breath to reset his focus before returning to his office and marketing meeting.

Later that afternoon, Dan and Reggie ducked out from work a little early. Over a couple beers, they had an interesting conversation about current events at Ark Technology Solutions.

***

That evening, Dan called Al. During a twenty-minute conversation, Dan alerted Al about the confrontation with Robert. He also relayed what Reggie told him about Robert preparing to hire a project manager. That part of the conversation angered Al almost as much as Robert had been earlier that day in the office hallway, although at least this time Dan was prepared for the reaction. Al let on that Robert called him twice already that afternoon, but had not left any voice messages.

"I'm out until Tuesday," Al explained. "Valerie and I are driving to the beach tomorrow for a long weekend. I will get with Robert when I come back," Al said. Dan was unsure if Al's tone indicated reassurance or resolution.

"What do you want me to do about the commission reduction?"

"We are reducing the commissions, Dan. That decision has been made. I appreciate why you gave Jessica a head's up, but that might have been a bit premature. Can you just hit pause on any further discussion around this until I get with Robert?"

"Yes I will. As for Jessica, I'm sorry about that. I was just trying to prepare her."

"I know, Dan. Don't worry about it. I will deal with Robert next week."

After the call, Dan realized that Al's last comment could be interpreted a number of ways. Which was correct, however, he was unsure.

***

Across town, Robert sat in bed reading when his phone chimed, indicating an incoming text message. He grabbed the phone off his nightstand, and, focusing on the bright screen, read:

Sorry I missed your calls today. Headed to the beach this weekend. Let's talk Tuesday morning. Have a few things to go over with you.

"What's that about?" Tess asked, having heard the chime.

"It's from Al."

"What's he want? It's unlike him to be working at this hour."

Robert chuckled darkly. "You're right. He's not working. He's at the beach."

"Is everything okay?"

"Yes," he scowled to himself. "It's just Al being Al."

Robert turned his phone to silent and set it back on the nightstand. He returned to his book but could not concentrate, finding that he was rereading the same few paragraphs over and over. Realizing his mind was elsewhere, Robert slammed the book shut, turned off his lamp, and rolled over, so angry he forgot to kiss Tess goodnight.

Week 5

"Hey, Robert—you got a few minutes? Can we talk?"

Robert looked up, shocked to see Al standing in his doorway. A quick glance to the wall clock revealed that it was not yet seven in the morning.

"Sure. What on earth are you doing here at this hour?"

"Hey, I can still get in early from time to time," Al said casually. "Besides, I wanted to get with you first thing after getting back into town." Al decided that coming to Robert's office early in the morning would be the best way to talk to his partner. Meeting in Robert's office would leave him feeling in control, and coming into the office early would demonstrate the importance Al placed on the issues that they needed to discuss.

"Okay . . ." Robert replied curiously. He motioned to the small conference table, grabbed his coffee mug, and joined Al at it. "Take a seat. What's up?"

"Thanks." Al sat at the table. "Did you have a good weekend?"

"Sure," Robert shrugged. "Fairly uneventful. Lots of kid activities."

"I remember those days. We had a good weekend too. The beach is still quiet this time of year, which we like."

Robert took a sip of coffee, made a show of examining a potential chip on the ceramic mug's rim, and then took another sip.

"Robert, we need to talk about what happened with you and Dan last week."

"Shoot."

"I am sorry that you got caught off guard. I did not realize that neither Dan nor I told you we made this change. However, you can't just march up and down the hallway, pulling people out of meetings when you are angry."

"Sounds like Dan came running to you."

"No, he did not come running to me. He did the right thing by coming to me in private and letting me know you were upset. That's the proper way to handle things like this."

"Are you here to scold me, Al?"

"No, Robert, I am not scolding you. I am pointing out as your partner the need for us to communicate when we disagree."

"This meeting is about communicating, then?"

"Yes, it is. Robert, I know you don't like the idea of cutting commissions on project work. But you don't need to worry about Jessica. Dan will make sure she doesn't experience any reduction in her compensation. It's important we make this change, though. We have to focus on service work to maximize the value for when we sell the company."

"I am not selling, Al."

"What are you talking about?"

"I am not selling my half of the business."

"But you agreed to sell."

"I never agreed to any such thing."

"Yes, you did. Are you forgetting? We met with an investment banker."

"I agreed to meet with you and the investment banker. I agreed to learn what our business might be worth. But I never agreed to sell."

"Well, you could have told me this a lot sooner."

"You could have *asked* me a lot sooner. Heck, you never even asked me if I wanted to sell. You just plowed forward, assuming I would because that's what you want."

"Robert, did you see the potential sale price that Taylor showed us? That's a lot of money. This is not just good for me. It's good for you, too, and our families."

"Oh? You want to bring up families now?"

"What are you talking about?"

"I'm talking about families. Specifically, mine."

"Okay . . . go on."

"Selling at the prices Taylor showed us is not good for my family. I still have three kids not yet in college. Even if we sold for the top price he showed us, I couldn't retire. I'd have to get a new job or stick around and work for the new owner. Who knows what the new owner would be like? I am not taking that risk.

"Also, my daughter works here. Remember her? She's my family. She wants this business one day, and I want her to have it. Selling this business denies her and me that future. So, contrary to what you just said, selling is not good for my family."

"You're worried about Jessica? Robert, she's in her twenties. She's incredibly talented. She can write a ticket anywhere."

"Yes, she can. But she does not want to be anywhere; she wants to be here. And I want to be here too, with her, for a long time to come."

"So, what's this mean? That I have to stick around because you and your daughter are attached to this place—a place that, need I remind you, I own more than half of?" Al asked, astounded that after all these years working together, Robert was seemingly putting his young daughter's career ahead of Al's needs.

"No, you don't have to stick around. I would prefer that you do, but if you want out, then I guess we'll need to buy you out."

"Really? Where will you get the millions of dollars, Robert? Please answer me that." Al steepled his fingers under his chin, mocking eagerness.

"We will pay you over time."

"Oh, that's rich. So let me get this straight. You want to block my ability to get paid millions of dollars in cash. Instead, I get to sell my half of the business for zero money down and the potentiality of collecting my money over what's likely to be many years. Is that right?"

"You don't know that it would be zero money down. We will be able to come up with something."

"You keep saying 'we.' Who's we?"

"Me, my daughter, and perhaps Jason Lee."

"This is getting better! I like this now. You're asking me to walk away from millions in cash and instead sell my business for probably very little money down, and my buyers are you, a twenty-something-year-old girl, and an employee that I barely know. Where do I sign?"

"The sarcasm isn't helping."

"Neither are the pie-in-the-sky ideas, Robert. I am not selling my business to you for less money than I could get if I sold it to an outsider. You can bank on that. Speaking of banks, that's what you will have to do, Robert. Go to the bank and borrow the money. You want this business? Fine. Buy it from me—with cash."

"You and I both know that my family could not afford to borrow that much money. Besides, the risks would be enormous."

"Wait. Hold on. You're angry with me because you feel like my desire to sell the business is hurting you and your family, but you sit here expecting me to walk away from millions, leaving me unable to retire with financial security for me and *my* family? Do you see the irony here, Robert?"

Both men sat thoughtfully, neither speaking for a moment. Robert meditated on the unjustness of Al expecting him to sell. Al grew indignant over his junior partner's apparent willingness to block his own exit success. His mind made up, Al told himself it was time to pull rank.

"Since we are thrashing things out, we are cutting the commission rates on project sales. That decision has been made, Robert. And you're not hiring a project manager. I am nixing that idea."

"What? Who do you think you are?"

"I am CEO. Our vice president of sales reports to me. As such, I ordered him to make this change."

"That's total bull. You're cutting commissions on project sales to reduce our project sales—"

"Yes I am, so that we get back to our core business, which is service work."

"You're living in the past, Al. The market has changed. Our customers expect us to do these projects. We can't just put our head in the sand and say, 'Sorry, we don't like doing projects as much as service work, so we won't do it for you.' Heck, you helped me sell our very first projects! Have you gotten so out of touch that you can't remember that? The fact is that project-related work is a big part of our present, and it needs to be an even bigger part of our future. You're making a decision that impacts me just as much as you, and that's not right."

Robert kept talking rapidly to prevent Al from getting a word in. "Furthermore, I *am* hiring a PM," he said, angrily putting his finger down on the table. "I have been hiring people here for seventeen years without your approval. I didn't need it before, and I don't need it now."

"You do need my agreement. With what money are you hiring this person? There's nothing in our budget for a project manager."

"Budget? What budget? That's a document we put together once per year and never look at. Be real. We have plenty of cash."

"That cash is owned by the company, which is fifty-one percent owned by me. You're not taking half of my cash to hire somebody."

"How are you going to stop me? Tell Reggie not to pay somebody that I have hired? That will play out well, Al. Dragging our employees into the middle of this is not the brightest idea."

"Look who's talking! That's exactly what you did last week when you threw a tantrum in the hallway where everybody could see and hear you. You have already dragged our people into this. That was a dumb move, Robert. You should have called me."

"I did call you—twice! You didn't return my calls, instead texting me later to let me know you'll get back to me when you are ready, after you sit on the beach for three or four days. Great leadership on your part, Al."

Robert's office phone rang. He let it ring until, after a seemingly interminable number of rings, the call finally went to voice mail.

When silence returned, Robert resumed. "I am not selling, Al."

"You can't block me from getting paid what this business is worth, Robert."

"I don't want to block you from getting anything. But you can't force me to sell, or go into millions of dollars in debt, just because you want your money."

"We are making the commission changes I ordered, Robert, and you're not hiring a project manager. So live with it."

"You're not a god around here, Al."

"No, I am not. But I am CEO and have been for seventeen years. If you don't like it, then you don't have to stay."

"Quit? I don't think so. You can't fire me either. So you had better find a way to live with including me on decisions like these."

"You're asking me if I think I'm a deity, yet you feel you cannot be fired? When did you become invincible?"

"I am an owner. You can't fire me. Even if you could, what are you going to fire me for? Have you seen our profits? We are at all-time record highs."

"We are at all-time highs doing the kind of work that we should not be doing."

"Where does it say that? Now you're changing the rules on me, Al— on all of us."

"If you want to look at it that way, that's fine. It is in my job description to change the rules when necessary."

"That's a good one. What job description? Can I read that, please?"

Exhausted, neither co-owner said anything. They looked at their hands, the table, anything but each other. After perhaps the longest fifteen seconds both men would ever experience, Robert finally spoke.

"What you want to happen will hurt me and my family, Al. I won't go for it."

"By not going for it, you are hurting me and my family, Robert. You can't deny that to me."

Robert's office phone commenced ringing again. This time, Robert walked to his desk and answered it, his back to Al. Recognizing the snub, Al wearily got up from the table and left Robert's office.

Later that afternoon,
Al's office at Ark Technology Solutions Inc.

"Al? It's Taylor Collins—did I catch you where you have a minute? I tried you a couple times recently, but your staff said you were at the beach." Taylor held a printout of Ark's reformatted income statement in his hand. Al e-mailed the document to him earlier last week.

"Hey, Taylor. Sure, now is as good a time as any, I guess. Robert and I were talking about you earlier this morning. Just let me close my door."

To Taylor's ears, Al sounded tired. He waited patiently, hearing some shuffling noises, before Al rejoined the line.

"Thanks for calling, Taylor. Did you have a chance to review the revised income statements I sent over? You should see the breakout of project revenue and service revenue."

"We got the statements. That's why I called. I have some questions. First, what did you do about your customers who use you for both types of work? I have in my notes that was an open issue when we met a couple weeks ago."

"It took us quite a bit of time, but we went back and reviewed all of our contracts and invoices, and separated out the two types of revenue. Plus, when new projects and service agreements come in, we will now code that revenue differently in our accounting system. That way we won't have this issue going forward."

"That's good, Al. All I have, however, is an income statement for this current year. Did you go back and break out the two types of work for the last three years?"

"What do you mean?"

"Well, a potential buyer is going to want an accurate picture of the company's financial performance for the past three years at a minimum, and preferably five." Taylor took a breath before asking his next question, afraid he already knew the answer. "Did you guys only sort out the two types of revenue with your current customers?"

"We went through all of our current customers and the few customers we have who terminated with us since the start of the year, as well. That gives an accurate picture of our revenue mix for this year.

Most of the terminated customers," Al explained, "were project customers whose work was successfully finished. I don't want you to think we are losing customers left and right or anything."

"I am sure you have good customer retention. That's not the issue. I see that you are doing a fairly considerable amount of project work, relative to the total. A potential buyer will want to see your prior results and trend line. That will require going back and breaking out the two revenue types across all your customers for at least the last three years. Having the information for just this year will not be sufficient, I'm afraid."

"Seriously? Taylor, that's quite a bit more work," Al said, exasperated. "I already pushed my team pretty hard to get you this data. Going back three years will require a lot more time and effort."

"I understand there is some work required, but you need to do this. It might not take as long as you think. A lot of your current service customers have been with you for the last three years, correct? You have already recoded the revenue for them. Now all you have to do is go back and recode the revenue for customers you had during the three prior years, but not with you now."

"Yes that's true, but it's still going to take some time."

Taylor waited, knowing the best thing he could say while that information set in was nothing.

"I don't know what to tell my team about this either," Al mused.

"What do you mean?"

"This is a lot of extra work for them. I was able to explain why we needed to recode our revenue for this year, so that going forward we had better data. But going back for three years, well, that's going to raise some eyebrows. I don't like being less than fully honest with my people."

Taylor was surprised that this issue had not come up already. Most owners were highly concerned about confidentiality. They wanted to tell as few employees as possible about a potential sale—preferably none. Getting a company ready for sale is a team effort, however, and difficult (if not impossible) to do without help from key members of the team.

"You haven't yet told anybody within the company that you are contemplating sale?"

"No. Only Robert and I know."

"Al, you have to tell your key leaders at some point. In my experience, if your top employees are trustworthy, and they trust you, they will be fine. Including them in the process works out better in the long run, for you and for them. I am not suggesting you confide in all of your people at this point, just your top leaders in important areas like your financial department."

"Okay. I guess we will have to figure something out."

Taylor waited again for Al to collect his thoughts before asking his next question. He knew to be careful to not pile onto owners at this stage of the process. "Al, have you talked with your accountants about getting your financial statements audited? That's another important area of getting ready to sell the business."

"No, Taylor. I've not had time. I've got to tell you, though, I am leery about the cost. I hear it's expensive."

"That's a common concern. However, having audited financial statements may actually help increase the price of the sale, because your potential buyer has accurate financial statements to evaluate. Additionally, having an audit typically shortens the due diligence period, reducing your risk and costs. It's an important step in getting ready to sell."

Taylor was pretty sure he heard a sigh on the other end of the phone.

"That's going to take even more time and money."

"Al, getting a business ready to sell is hard work for most owners. You can see now why most owners end up wishing they started much earlier preparing for exit. It takes a lot of time and effort. Rushing things at the end rarely works out well. It makes things harder, riskier, more expensive, and more stressful.

"I am not telling you these things to discourage you. I have learned it's better to get the bad news on the table and dealt with upfront. It makes things easier as we go. I feel we can help you and Robert get the best price for your business when you sell. However, your business is not ready for sale yet. You stand to gain a substantially better result if you take the time to properly prepare yourselves and your company.

"I have somebody you should meet. This person helps business owners get ready for exit. His name is James Rigney. He and his team actually do the work of helping you and your team prepare the company for sale, far beyond what we are equipped to do. I also know he helps business partners figure out how to exit successfully, when one partner might have a different set of goals than another." Taylor waited to see if that last comment would generate any noticeable reaction. It did not.

"Let me put you in touch with him. I'd recommend you at least sit down with them and learn what they do. It could greatly benefit you, your partner, and your company."

Al's answer surprised him. "Okay, Taylor, perhaps you're right. I think I have already heard from this guy from another source. You can have him call me."

Taylor stared at the phone for a minute after ending the call. He wished he had a dollar for every time he had to deliver bad news to a business owner. It would add up to a nice stream of money, he thought, although it wouldn't be much fun.

***

The next two weeks passed slowly and stressfully for both co-owners.

During the first week, both men went out of their way to avoid seeing the other, all without consciously admitting to themselves that they were doing anything out of the ordinary. This proved to be simple at first. Take a different hallway if one suspected the other man was walking about. Depart for lunch early and alone to avoid the risk of being invited out for a group lunch at which the other could be present. Grab some work files and leave early. Sneak a glance out the window at the employee parking lot to see if the other man already left. Feign a conflict and bow out of a meeting that the other would be attending. Shoot off an e-mail to the other man on a topic that would best be discussed on the phone or in person. Before either knew it, five days passed with no apparent ill effects.

By the next week, keeping up appearances was proving more difficult. Al found himself driving into work a little later each day with a growing feeling of anxiety as he got closer to their office. He noticed he ate less during the day. His wife noticed he consumed an additional glass of wine—or two—in the evening. Robert, meanwhile, found himself driving to work even earlier than usual, to justify to himself why he could leave before the day was barely half over. When he was at the office, for the first time in his career, Robert worked behind a closed door.

During that second week, Ark's employees began to notice something was wrong. Business projects that required both partners' attention stalled. E-mails to their bosses went unanswered or were returned with curt, uninformative responses. Invitations extended to both men to discuss a pressing matter were declined by at least one and sometimes both, usually with an explanation of an overlapping appointment despite the fact that the shared online calendar showed no such conflict. Late arrivals, early departures, and closed doors became the subject of break-room discussions.

Midway through the third week, Al surprised Valerie with the suggestion that they drop everything and drive to Birmingham for a long weekend visit with their daughter and her family. They had a fine trip, and drove back to Atlanta on Sunday evening.

As Al drove, Valerie put down the magazine she was reading and turned to him. "If you are not going to tell me what is wrong, then please solve it quickly."

"What?" Al asked his wife, entirely caught off guard by the question.

"Clearly something is bothering you. Don't try to tell me otherwise. You've been sullen for weeks now. Even your daughter asked me about it this weekend. So, either share it with me or fix it. What do you always tell our daughters? 'Are you working the problem or the solution?'"

Al kept his eyes on the road, but out of his peripheral vision he saw Valerie resume looking at her magazine. She said her piece and expected him to honor it. He loved her very much.

That night, Al barely slept. At three a.m. he was wide awake in bed, staring at the shadows dancing across his bedroom ceiling. He arose, quietly left the bedroom, and made to their den. There, he opened up the computer, logged into his e-mail, and sent the following message:

> *Robert,*
>
> *I think it's safe to say that both of us are unhappy with this situation. I also think it's worth talking to somebody who maybe could help. Both Linda Hamill and Taylor Collins recommended somebody for us to talk to—ironically, it was the same guy. Let's sit down with this person. If he can help us, great. If not, we haven't lost anything.*
>
> *I'll have our assistant set up a meeting for us with him. Btw his name is James Rigney. I have not spoken to him myself.*
>
> *Al*

Al turned off the computer and made his way back to bed. Within minutes, he was asleep.

***

Less than an hour later, Robert sat down at his desk in Ark's offices and logged onto his computer. As was his custom, he opened his e-mail first to check on any pressing matters. To his surprise, an e-mail from Al appeared to have been sent just a short while earlier. Robert, a feeling of wariness settling over him, read it.

Robert's initial reaction was to fire back a reply telling Al that he would not meet with somebody whom Al had found. Yet as his fingers positioned on the keyboard, he paused. He had to admit that Al was right; neither of them was happy with the state of things. Even though Linda Hamill was Al's relationship, Robert met the CEO Group Chair on many occasions and had no reason to mistrust her. Taylor Collins seemed like a knowledgeable investment banker. If both Linda and Taylor recommended the same person, then he was willing to try. Thus, Robert changed his mind. He hit the reply button and typed the following response:

OK.

Week 9

Wednesday, 10:00 a.m.,
in the offices of Ark Technology Solutions Inc.

"Al? Robert? Good to meet you both. I am James Rigney."

James shook hands with both men and followed as they led him into a company conference room. Once in the room, Robert retrieved several bottles of water from a refrigerator installed under a side countertop, kept one, then put the rest in the center of the conference table and took a seat. Al refilled the coffee mug he carried with him into the room. Eventually, all three men took seats at the table. Al sat at the head of the table, and Robert took an empty chair two seats removed further down. James noticed that neither man made eye contact with the other. James intentionally sat on the opposite side so he could see both men at the same time.

James waited a moment to see if either man would speak first. Neither said a word. One did not need James's more than twenty-five years' experience working with business owners to sense the tension in the room. This would not be fun.

Sales meetings were not James's favorite activity. It wasn't that he was bad at selling; his results confirmed he was actually quite effective. He simply did not like meeting with people who did not yet know him, and thus had no reason to trust him or his motives. To reframe his aversion to sales, long ago he decided that he would treat prospects such as these two men as if they already were clients, giving them right upfront his best ideas and recommendations. That way he could focus on being a consultant, and only rarely have to act as a salesperson. Over time, he came to see that the better, longer-term clients hired him anyway because

101

they didn't want to do things themselves and saw value in a relationship with him.

He had no idea if these two men would ever be clients. Their tenseness suggested odds were not good. James gritted his teeth in silent resolve and got started.

"It's good to meet you both. I know little about you and your company, but you must be doing a lot of things right. Two people that I hold in high regard, Linda Hamill and Taylor Collins, said good things about you and Ark."

"That's nice to hear," Al said noncommittally. Robert said nothing.

"I'd like to hear more about you and your company, but out of courtesy let me introduce myself and explain what my firm does. Do you have any objection?" James intentionally phrased his question so that the desired answer was "no." People in defensive moods—and these two business co-owners appeared shut off at this point—were usually more comfortable saying no than yes. Al answered with a clear "no" while Robert mumbled what sounded like "nope."

"Briefly, my firm helps business owners plan for and achieve successful exits," James began. "Business owners typically have the majority of their net worth tied up in their business, and therefore need to exit successfully to achieve personal financial freedom. It's not just about money, however. Most owners have nonfinancial goals they want to achieve at exit, such as making sure the company continues forward in good hands and exiting on their own terms."

James then shared a quick summary of his background and experience to establish some level of credibility. He was eager to get these two talking not just to him, but more importantly to each other.

"The fact that Taylor and Linda recommended me to you tells me that you have had at least *some* conversations about the issue of exit. Would either of you bring me up to speed as to where you are on this subject?"

For the first time, the two co-owners looked at each other, apparently to determine who would speak first. Robert's stony eyes indicated he expected Al to answer.

"We've only had a few discussions up to this point," Al began. "We've been partners for seventeen years. We feel we built something special here." James began taking notes in his portfolio. "We met with Taylor to learn what our company might be worth at sale."

James waited, unsure if Al was unable or unwilling to say more. Seeing that he was not going to say anything further, James picked up the conversation.

"Meeting with an investment banker like Taylor can be a valuable exercise," he acknowledged. "While the numbers Taylor gave you are only an estimate, it's helpful to know what your company could be worth in the marketplace. Now, when two co-owners equally own a business, often they—"

"I own fifty-one percent," Al interrupted.

Robert cleared his throat.

"Oh, thanks for letting me know." James made another note on his pad. While writing, he elected to avoid any further discussion of ownership, at least for now. "Back to the issue of the market-value estimate you received from Taylor. May I guess how you reacted to the figures? I'll bet that one of you would jump at the chance to sell the business for that amount, and one of you would not."

"Yes, that's true," Al offered.

"May I venture another guess? One of you would love to sell the business, and one of you would not."

"Yes, that's true too," Al replied hesitantly. James was pleased to observe the other man straighten up in curiosity.

"Let me try one more," he continued. "One of you wants to exit sooner, and the other does not want to exit at this time."

Al smiled. "You're three for three."

"So you're a magical mindreading exit planner?" Robert asked James snidely. It was the first thing Robert said to him since shaking hands. "Can you tell which one of us wants to sell now and which does not?"

James was not exactly sure of the answer to Robert's question, but his odds were at worst fifty-fifty, and he had a pretty good idea. Feigning more certainty than he felt, James answered, "Sure, Robert. You don't want to sell. Al does."

"Either Linda or Taylor must have told you all of this," Robert said dismissively.

James shook his head. "Both said that you two might use my help, but neither offered any specifics."

"Then how," Al asked, checking his watch, "did you figure out all of this in under ten minutes without asking us any questions?"

"There's no magic involved. I admit that I don't always get all of my guesses right, but it would have been notable if I had gotten more than one question wrong. You see, I knew your answers, well at least your likely answers, before I ever met you."

"Care to explain?" Al asked curiously.

"Sure. To do that, we first need to take a step back. We need to talk about the importance of getting your exit right. Any objection?"

Al and Robert looked at each other. James thought he saw a smile pass between them. Good.

"No. Please proceed," Al replied, genuinely interested.

"Initially, many owners do not cherish thinking about and working on their exit. Some view exit as the end of a journey they would prefer not finish. If you are happy and successful, why bother to plan your exit? Nobody wants to exit from a happy marriage or a rewarding friendship.

"However, exit is inevitable. Even if you prefer to work until your health and life are exhausted, all owners still must address how their exit impacts family, employees, customers, and the business legacy. Your future exit deserves your present attention. Undoubtedly you have worked too hard and accomplished too much to surrender control over the eventual outcome. Failing to plan ahead risks denying yourself the chance to achieve a successful exit and denies others the chance to share in that success with you."

"We feel proud and blessed to have a successful business," Al shared. "Robert and I both want those things you mentioned. We both want to be financially secure and make sure this business goes on without us. That's not the problem. As you already guessed, I want to exit sometime soon. Robert does not. I want to sell the business now. He does not. That's why we agreed to meet with you. Where does that leave us?"

"Great question. It leaves you two bound together by the Three-Link Chain."

"The what?" Robert asked skeptically.

"The Three-Link Chain. Imagine a chain with three links. Each link has a sentence printed on it. The first link says, 'Business owners cannot achieve their major goals without a successful exit.' That's what I just talked about. Your financial security, the freedom to do what you want to do, and your desire to create a sustainable business—all of these things you probably cannot achieve without a successful exit."

Al and Robert unconsciously nodded in agreement.

James continued, "The second link says, 'Business co-owners cannot successfully exit if their goals are incompatible with one another.' It would seem that you two gentlemen have already discovered the second link. Al, your desire to sell the business now at its current value is incompatible with Robert's desire to wait and sell the business later for a greater amount."

"No, that's not correct," Robert interrupted. "I mean, it is correct that I don't want to exit now, and I wouldn't sell my half for what the company is apparently worth today. But I don't want to sell the business at all. I want to pass it down to my daughter. She works here."

"I have not had a chance to ask either of you about your individual exit goals, so I didn't know about her," James replied. "It seems your exit goals are even less compatible. Let me get this right. Al, you want to sell now at the company's current value. Robert, you want to keep working for now and at some point give it to your daughter. Do I have that correct?"

"Yes," Robert answered impatiently.

"Can I assume," James resumed, "that you two have discussed the rather obvious solution—Robert, you buy out Al?"

The two business co-owners nodded their heads in unison.

"Neither of you likes that idea, right?"

The nodding heads quickly switched to shaking heads. "Too much risk the way Al wants it," Robert said grimly.

"Too little cash," Al said, only a half step behind Robert.

"Your concerns about a partner buyout are quite common. As I said, you're already shackled by the second link of the Three-Link Chain. Again, the second link says, 'Business co-owners cannot successfully exit if their exit goals are incompatible with one another.'

"That takes us to the third chain link. It says, 'Goal compatibility can only be achieved with a conscious and ongoing effort to create co-owner alignment.' Your impasse will not go away on its own. These issues don't cure themselves with time. If anything, waiting makes matters worse, because with less time you will have fewer solutions. Therefore, ultimately if you two gentlemen each want to exit successfully one day, you have a lot of work to do. That's why it's called the Three-Link Chain. You, gentlemen, are bound together in this."

James let what he had covered set in. After a silence, Robert surprised James by speaking next.

"I guess that makes sense, James," Robert began. "I have been pretty upset about this for the last few weeks now. I almost did not agree to attend this meeting. I don't understand why after seventeen years together, seemingly overnight Al and I are now clashing about this stuff and not getting along."

"Thank you for admitting that," James replied warmly. "These issues can be difficult. Your incompatible goals have nothing to do with the quality of your relationship, or how long you have been business partners. No matter how well you two worked together up to this point, nor for how long, it's no surprise that you ended up here. Business co-owners having incompatible goals at exit is almost inevitable."

"Why is that? We've enjoyed a solid relationship until now," Al added. "We built a great business together. Unlike a lot of other partnerships, we usually get along well. But things have been rough lately. It feels like something changed."

"That's because something did change. Your goals changed."

Al and Robert looked at James, confusion spread across their faces.

"For seventeen years," James continued, "you have been two co-owners seeking to build a business together. This shared goal kept you in a high state of alignment with each other. Sure, you may have disagreed from time to time about how to best grow your business, but you both ultimately wanted the same thing. Now, each of you wants something different. Al, you don't want to build a business anymore. Rather, you want to exit from a business. Robert, you don't want to build a business with just Al anymore. Rather, you want to build a business that includes your daughter. The moment your goals changed, you stopped being in alignment with each other. As soon as you were no longer in alignment with each other, you found yourselves wondering what's gone wrong with the other guy."

Al and Robert chuckled in embarrassed recognition.

"It's good to laugh a bit at this," James conceded, smiling himself. "What you are experiencing is, like I said, practically inevitable—for you and for most business co-owners. Had you been partners together for another seventeen years, likely this still would have happened. Having incompatible exit goals occurs because you are different people with different wants, circumstances, and opportunities.

"Let me ask you some questions. You are different ages, yes?"

"Yes," Al answered. "I am ten years older."

"Right, and Al, you want to exit sooner largely because of this age difference. Here's another question. Al, you said you would sell your half of the business for the estimated valuation that Taylor gave you. Robert, you said that even if you wanted to sell, you could not sell at that price. Robert, do you have children? Are they still young?"

"I have four kids—my daughter Jessica, who works here, from my first marriage, and three children in my second. My three younger kids range from eighteen down to eleven."

"Thanks, Robert." James turned to Al. "I am inferring from your age that any children you have are grown and no longer dependent on you, yes?"

Al nodded.

"Right. While I know nothing about your personal financial situation, it's very likely that, Robert, you would need a lot more money from a sale at this stage in your life because your family costs are much higher — a second marriage, younger children, and so on. All of that translates into each of you needing a different amount at exit to reach personal financial freedom. That, too, is common among co-owners.

"Robert, you already mentioned your daughter's involvement in the business. Al, do you have any children who work here or may want to work here?"

"No, I don't."

"So there's a third difference between you two. You have a different number of family members working in the business. That reality can cause exit goals to diverge.

"Do you see how your conflicting goals were almost bound to occur? Incompatibility has nothing to do with how well you get along or how many years you've been together. It occurs simply because you are two different people. That's it. And since no two business co-owners are exact clones, having some incompatible goals at exit happens nearly all the time."

James waited a moment, respecting that the two other men were alone in their thoughts. Eventually, both men made eye contact with him, silently telling him to resume.

"Do you know what makes all of this even more ironic? The more you grow your company, the potentially worse the incompatibility gets."

"Is meeting with you always such a downer?" Robert asked.

"I hope not," James replied, ignoring the sarcasm. "My goal is not to be negative. My intention is to educate you on what you are experiencing and why it is happening. Otherwise, you'll find it harder to work through this."

"Let him speak," Al instructed Robert. James felt some of the tension return to the room with Robert's question and Al's rebuke. He quickly pressed forward.

"It helps to know that having incompatible goals at exit commonly occurs. It also helps to understand that the more successful your business, the more divergent your goals can become. There are several reasons for this. First, as your business's revenue, profits, and surplus cash increase, different co-owners often develop different ideas about what to do with the increased financial resources. For example, if the business has a spare million dollars lying around, one co-owner may want to take it out of the business, while another co-owner may want to reinvest for growth. Neither is right nor wrong; they just have different goals. Contrast that to a company that is small and not yet profitable. Its co-owners usually are in strong alignment that they must focus on growing the company—they usually don't have any other choice."

James noticed that Al and Robert exchanged a guarded look between themselves. They offered no explanation, however, so he continued.

"The second reason why increased business success adds to the likelihood for incompatible exit goals has to do with the number of employees and the job specialization that ensues. As most businesses grow, they employ more people, and those employees specialize. Contrast that with a very small business, such as a start-up. Its co-owners typically must be jacks-of-all-trades, taking turns doing anything and everything to grow the business. Later, once the business reaches a larger size with more employees, then the co-owners working in that business will specialize just like the other employees."

"Remember those days?" Al asked his partner. "We used to do everything at the company. Now, I sometimes feel like I hardly know how anything works around here. But how does the job specialization contribute to incompatible goals at exit?"

"As the co-owners working in the business specialize," James explained, "they take on different roles and responsibilities. Some roles are more stressful, and some demand longer hours. Some roles are easier to replace at exit, and some are more difficult to transition and replace. These differences can contribute to the co-owners having different goals at exit. Some co-owners will be eager to exit or make a quick transition. Other co-owners may be less eager to exit or may desire to remain with the company in some capacity even after exit. The differences in roles and responsibilities influence different goals at exit."

James paused ostensibly to open a water bottle and take a drink. Actually, he wanted to pause for questions or comments. When none came, he continued.

"The third and final way that business success can contribute to co-owners having incompatible goals at exit is simply that the number of co-owners likely increases. As a company gets bigger and older, the number of co-owners typically increases. Over time, families may pass ownership to siblings, children, cousins, and grandchildren. Perhaps key employees receive ownership, either as an incentive or by buying into the business. The more successful the business, the more likely some or all of these opportunities for additional co-owners occurs. All of this matters because as the number of co-owners increases, the potential for incompatible goals greatly increases."

"We are already seeing this happen within our company," Robert remarked.

"We are?" Al asked.

"Yes, we are," Robert said thinly. Turning to James, he explained, "We recently had a key employee approach us about buying into Ark. We haven't done anything yet about his inquiry, but we can't just leave him hanging. Plus, I want my daughter to have some ownership in the company. Add those together and we could increase from two to four co-owners in the foreseeable future."

"Let's not get ahead of ourselves, Robert," Al replied quickly. "I have not agreed to any changes in this company's ownership. We must first—"

"I am not getting ahead of anything," Robert interrupted angrily. "My daughter is the reason I am sitting here, Al."

Al said nothing in reply. Instead, he turned to James. "I don't get something. You make it sound as though every set of business co-owners hits a wall like we apparently have. Well, that's just not the case. I rarely hear about co-owners dealing with these issues."

"Good point, Al. I said several times today that goal incompatibility at exit among co-owners is common, perhaps even inevitable. You may not hear about it often, though. Many co-owners will not know goal incompatibility exists until they get close to exit. It sounds like you and Robert have had incompatible exit goals for some time now, but only recently are you openly talking about it. Then, once co-owners realize they face this issue, it's not a topic they readily want to admit to outsiders. Nobody wants their customers, employees, competitors, or peers to know these challenges are happening."

"Makes sense, James," Al said. "But still, not all business co-owners have completely opposite goals like Robert and I do."

"No, not all co-owners face as difficult a scenario as you two. Goal incompatibility at exit comes in degrees. Some business co-owners have exit goals which are only partially conflicting, while others are completely incompatible. Regardless, undesirable things happen. Goal incompatibility can cause strained or even broken relationships among co-owners, stunted business growth, legal confrontations, and ultimately failed exits."

"Cheery stuff, James," Robert said flatly.

The room became silent again. James looked at his phone to check the time. There was now less than fifteen minutes remaining in the time Al and Robert allotted for this meeting, but James had more ground to cover. Plus, he was not certain how much more these two co-owners were ready and willing to hear. Some of what they needed to hear would likely be even less cheery. James chose to let them decide the next step.

"Gentlemen, you're asking great questions, and I'm doing my best to answer them. However, what I still need to cover with you will take longer than the time we originally booked for this meeting. I can make myself available to stay, but I don't know if you can or want to at this point. What should we do?"

Al and Robert looked at each other once again. Robert deferred to Al as he had before.

"I am good for time," Al answered. "I suggest we take a quick break and then continue. Robert, is that okay with you?"

"You're asking for my input? Sure, Al. The guy is sitting here," Robert said, gesturing toward James. "I say we plow through this."

Al grabbed his empty coffee mug and walked out of the conference room. Robert stood, stretched, and quickly glanced at his phone before putting it away. When it appeared Robert was not going to leave the room, James decided to take advantage of having the one business co-owner alone.

"You're bothered, Robert," James said directly. "Bothered not just by the incompatible goals, but by something else."

Robert appeared taken aback. He seemed to weigh his response before finally replying, "You could say that," in a guarded manner.

"Why?"

"Shouldn't I be bothered?"

"I don't know. I don't know enough about your company or the two of you to know if you should or should not be."

"Well, I am. What Al is doing is wrong." Robert sat back down.

"How is Al's desire to sell wrong?"

"It's not that."

"Then what is wrong?"

Robert sat, thinking. James did not know if Robert was trying to come up with what to say or debating with himself whether he should say it.

"Al made his decision without ever talking to me. We are supposed to be partners. This is a big-deal issue. It impacts him, me, our company, my family, everybody. I have a right to have a say in these things. He never even told me he was thinking about selling. He only told me after his mind was made up."

"Do you believe he intentionally kept you in the dark?" James asked.

"Probably not. I mean, I trust him, so no, I don't believe that."

"Then why do you believe that he made his decision without talking to you?"

"Do you want me to answer that honestly?"

"Of course."

"I believe that he does not respect me enough. Yes, we act as equal partners—most of the time. But here, perhaps because he is older and has an extra two percent of the company, he felt he could decide this without me."

James carefully chose his next words. "I don't know what you guys talked about or did not talk about prior to today. I do know that if you feel left out of the decision-making process Al used to set his own business exit goals, then that's important. Business co-owners should consult with one another on these issues—early and often."

"Thank you," Robert said somewhat righteously.

"May I be blunt, Robert?"

"Absolutely," Robert answered excitedly, clearly expecting James to further dissect Al's behavior and shortcomings.

"Did you tell Al that you wanted to pass your interest in Ark to your daughter before or after you made your decision?"

"No, that's not the same thing," he replied vigorously. "My daughter has been here for five years. Five years! Anybody could figure it out that I want her to have the business one day. Heck, I have had employees come to me and tell me that they know she will be an owner in the future. If employees can figure that out for themselves, then Al could too."

"Maybe you're right. I certainly agree that people could deduce that you would want to pass your interest in the business to your daughter. However, I know many business owners who have a child or children working inside the company but don't plan on giving the business to them. It's not an automatic assumption.

"Let me ask another question. Does Al work with Jessica?"

"Not directly, why?"

"If he does not work directly with her, then how well does he know her?"

"He's known her since she was a teenager. He knows she's a real go-getter. He knows that she's become our top salesperson before turning thirty."

"That's not enough."

"Huh?"

"Al has known her since she was a child, and knows she's a young sales star. That's not the same as knowing her as a future owner in this business. Is Jessica entitled to ownership simply because she's your daughter?"

"Not at all. She's earned it."

"Says who? What Ark ownership training program did she complete? What Ark ownership requisite accomplishments did she fulfill?"

"We don't have anything that formal. We are a small company here."

"I know. Yet you are saying that she 'earned' becoming an owner. That's your conclusion. When did Al have any input on this? When has Al had a chance to evaluate her merits as a future owner? When did you and Al discuss and determine the criteria for somebody to join you as another co-owner within this business?"

"Are you saying my daughter does not deserve it?" Robert asked heatedly.

"No, Robert, I am not. Please relax. I am not saying she is or is not deserving of ownership. I don't know her. What I am saying is that you reached your own conclusions about her future with this company apparently without much input from Al. Bluntly, Robert, it sounds like both of you are making decisions without talking enough to each other."

James let those points settle. He was thankful Al had not yet returned to the room, but he did not know how much more private time with Robert he had left.

"Is it possible you are being too hard on Al? I agree that Al could have asked you for input before he finalized his exit goals. That likely would have been better. You could have asked Al for input before setting some of your goals. That likely would have been better too. You said that because Jessica has worked here for years, it should be obvious that you intend to pass your interest in the business to her. Maybe that's a fair point. But Al does not have any children working here. Plus, he's in his sixties, right? Isn't it just as possible to say that it should be apparent that Al would want to sell sometime soon? The things that Al has done—and not done—that have made you angry, haven't you acted in a similar manner?"

Robert sat silently. James readied another question. Before he could ask, Al walked back in the room.

"Well, it looks like you two have become fast friends," Al said teasingly upon reentering the room.

Confused at first, James realized that, to Al, it appeared that he and Robert sat silently at the table during the break.

"Well," James replied, "maybe not fast friends. But I have enjoyed getting to know Robert and his family a little bit better."

Turning back to Robert, James said, "Thank you for telling me more about Jessica. It must be a special opportunity and feeling to work with your daughter this way."

Robert looked up and, after a moment, smiled at James.

Al looked confused.

"Should we resume?" James asked, retaking control of their discussion. "We still have a lot to cover."

"Sure. We're following you," Robert replied attentively, to James's surprise.

"Okay. Now that you know what exit-goal incompatibility is, and you've recognized that it exists here, let's talk about how to deal with it. First, you need to know that resolving goal incompatibility and creating co-owner exit alignment is difficult. There are several reasons for this." James noticed that Robert took out a pen and opened his pad to take notes. Al also noticed and followed suit.

"First, to create co-owner alignment, all the co-owners involved have to clearly state and communicate their desires at exit. This may sound easier than it actually is. Many owners are not able to state their exit desires, only because they have not yet figured them out. Even if you have clearly figured out what your individual desires are, sharing them with your co-owners can feel selfish or disloyal. You have to be willing to say, 'Here's what I want at my exit . . .' and co-owners may struggle with this.

"A second reason why co-owners struggle to create exit alignment is the fear that talking about this stuff will cause tension or stress in the co-owners' relationship. It's the old adage about not rocking the boat. I think you gentlemen have discovered for yourselves that not talking about this stuff is usually worse than worrying about keeping the boat steady. I am glad for you that you are past that.

"There are several other reasons why many co-owners procrastinate or delay in addressing this issue, but again, you are already facing things, so let me jump ahead to the last major reason why creating co-owner exit alignment is difficult. Most co-owners make this harder on themselves."

Al and Robert looked up questioningly from their note-taking.

"Yes, you heard me. You may be making this harder on yourselves. I am not trying to scold you. Rather, I am sharing with you what you need to hear, even if it's uncomfortable."

"Would you explain, please?" Robert asked.

"Sure. Within many companies, the co-owners do things—or fail to do certain things—that, unbeknownst to them, undermine co-owner exit alignment. These things are usually habits, processes, and decisions that seem harmless or even virtuous today, but as exit draws near, they inhibit alignment. Thus, we call these 'Alignment Inhibitors.' The more Alignment Inhibitors occurring within a company, the more difficult creating and maintaining co-owner exit alignment becomes.

"Let's try an exercise to give you an example of an Alignment Inhibitor. Both of you, please write down on a piece of scratch paper your answer to the following question. What is the most important thing we need to do in our business today? Please keep your answer private."

James gave each man about ten seconds to write down his own answer, then collected the scratch paper from both. Opening Al's first, he read aloud:

Diversify our business mix and
accelerate the growth of our core service business.

James then took Robert's paper, and read aloud:

Expand our ability to sell and
execute more project-related work.

James held up a hand to prevent either man from speaking. "I suspect you both want to tell me why your answer is right. Let's table that for now. I am confident you both have strong reasons. What's important is that your answers are different. Can you see that?"

"Yes," both men said in unison.

"Me too," James said. "How do your answers align with your company's written strategic growth plan?"

"We don't have one," Robert answered. "We feel long-term business planning is a waste of time. Not for everybody, but for us. Our market moves too fast. We need to be nimble. So you know, we achieved significant business growth over the years without doing formal written plans."

"While I think there are powerful advantages to doing long-term strategic planning," James replied, "I accept that you have grown your business without a written strategic plan up to this point. However, while it's possible to grow your business for many years without long-term strategic planning, it's difficult to create co-owner alignment and exit success without it. Let me explain why.

"Consider your different answers to the question I posed. Al wants to grow the business one way, and Robert, you want to grow it a completely different way. Likely neither of you is right nor wrong. You are, however, rowing your boat in two different directions. That's a setup to go nowhere."

"Wait," Al jumped in. "To create a written document called a 'strategic plan,' or whatever you want to call it, Robert and I still would have to thrash out our different points of view. It's not like having a written document miraculously brings us into alignment."

"Exactly!" James said enthusiastically. "The written document doesn't create alignment, but rather the process you go through to create the document creates alignment. To produce a strategic plan, you two have to 'thrash out' your different views and figure out together how to best grow this business. That's what an effective strategic planning process requires. The alternative is you each try to outmaneuver each other and implement your own ideas faster than the other guy can implement his.

"Not doing long-term strategic planning, and therefore not having a written document which encapsulates your plan, is an Alignment Inhibitor. The document captures your decisions, strategies, and tactics so that both of you and your team agree and know what is to be done. Not having the long-term plan can undermine alignment while you are growing your business. It absolutely will make creating alignment difficult when one or both of your goals change and your focus shifts on how to successfully exit from the business."

"Okay, I get it," Robert commented. "I can see where Al and I are not on the same page and have been working against one another's efforts. As much as I shudder to ask, what's another example of an Alignment Inhibitor?"

"If you gentlemen are up for it, here's one that can be tough to talk about. How do you know if the other is doing a good job?"

"We just know," Al answered. "We have worked together side by side at this company for close to twenty years."

"Do you each have job descriptions? With performance benchmarks that you periodically review and update?" James followed up.

"We don't need anything that formal," Al answered.

"Do your employees have written job descriptions?"

"Sure," Al said slowly, unsure where this line of questioning was going.

"How come your employees have job descriptions, but you two do not?"

Al hesitated. "Because we are the company's owners," he eventually said.

"But you work here as employees too," James countered. "Why have you exempted yourselves from one of the basic tools of managing employees?"

"We use job descriptions to make sure our employees are doing their jobs well," Al said, as if the answer should be obvious. "We are not worried about whether or not we are doing our own jobs well. It's our company, after all."

"All right, let's test this," James replied. "Al, let me ask you—is Robert doing his job perfectly?"

Al started to speak, then wavered as if changing his answer. "No, he isn't. But nobody is perfect."

"I agree that nobody is perfect," James said, nodding in affirmation. "Robert—can you and I also agree that Al is not doing his job perfectly either?"

"Yes, I agree," Robert replied without hesitation.

"Good. All of us agree that neither of you is perfect. It also seems that both of you have some thoughts about how the other person could potentially improve their job performance, even if only modestly. Now, when was the last time you two sat down together, openly discussed and reviewed your job performance, and then created or updated specific, measurable benchmarks for the job that person occupies?"

Al and Robert exchanged glances, confusion apparent on their faces. Then Al answered, "I don't know if we've ever done that. But frankly, I don't see the need. We talk all the time."

"I am sure you talk often," James acknowledged, "but let me ask you, Al, how can Robert maximize his job performance if you don't specifically and objectively give him input and suggestions from time to time? Also Al, how can you be sure that you and Robert are in agreement—and agreement is another word for alignment—about the exact performance that the company needs from the job Robert occupies? Al, you may feel that Robert needs to do more of X and less of Y, while Robert may feel the exact opposite. There's no way to know unless you talk it through, set clear goals in writing, and periodically compare performance against those goals. And the exact same questions apply to Al's performance as well, Robert."

"James," Al said somewhat impatiently, "I think you're being unrealistic. Robert and I are partners. We treat each other as equals. Do you know how hard it is to walk into your partner's office and say, 'Hey, I think you could do a better job here'?"

"Yes, I know exactly how hard that would be. It is so hard because it's the wrong way to give feedback to somebody. Let's stop and think about this. You two are likely the most important employees here, and you both make the decisions that have the biggest impact on the company. Yet neither of you has any clearly defined, written, actively reviewed job performance goals and results. Is that the best way to do things? Also, how much harder is it for two or more co-owners to stay in alignment with each other when everybody's job description and performance benchmarks only exist in everybody's heads?

"Of *course* it would be hard to just walk into each other's office and say, 'Hey, let's talk about your performance.' So you don't do it that way. You use tools to put a structure and process to this so that the conversations can happen constructively. Those tools include written job descriptions, periodic performance evaluations, and ultimately, compensation plans tied to that job and job performance—not tied to the ownership level. Not having those tools is another Alignment Inhibitor. Without them, there is a much higher risk of co-owners innocently and unknowingly rowing the boat in different directions."

After an uncomfortable silence, James said, "Look, gentlemen. I appreciate that it's not much fun to have somebody like me sit here and point out mistakes. But it's better to know about the problems so you can deal with them than to continue feeling pain and stress and not know why."

"We are big boys, James," Al said defensively. "It sounds like we have some bad habits here, ones that have been in place for quite a while. But I am not sure that I agree with you that our problems will go away if we have business plans and job descriptions."

"That's not what I am saying," James corrected. "Your problems don't go away if you have these things in place. The problems you and Robert have are rooted in your incompatible exit goals. What I am saying is that you, like most business co-owners, likely are making it harder to address your incompatible exit goals because there are certain things you are doing and not doing that inhibit your efforts to be in alignment. Creating co-owner alignment at exit when you have incompatible goals is difficult to do. By addressing and, where possible, eliminating these inhibitors, you can make it easier on yourselves to reach alignment. Notice that I said 'easier.' That does not mean easy."

"You seem to be making a lot of good guesses about us," Robert commented. "You're not clairvoyant. That must mean the things we are doing—and not doing—which undermine alignment are common mistakes?"

"Yes, and it's important to understand why. It's possible to grow a business without formal business planning and job descriptions. You've proven it. Many other business owners have accomplished something similar. But we are not talking about the best ways to grow your business. We are talking about how to successfully exit from a business. Those are two different things.

"Alignment Inhibitors are common. We have identified six that frequently occur in small to midsized companies. I suspect we don't want to go through the full list today. After today's meeting, I will provide you with a document called 'The Guide to Creating Co-Owner Exit Alignment,' which, as its name suggests, will cover in detail all the Alignment Inhibitors, as well as the rest of what we talk about today. May I suggest that, in the interest of time, we move forward and talk about how to actually achieve co-owner alignment?"

"Sure, that makes sense," Robert agreed, not looking to Al for confirmation. "Let's talk about where we go from here."

***

"To start, business co-owners need to develop alignment around the Five Major Exit Goals. Before we explore the Five Goals, let's quickly define what we mean when we say 'alignment' in this context. Alignment does not mean matching or identical. Co-owners can have different exit goals and plans. Alignment simply means co-owners' goals will not undermine or interfere with another co-owner's exit goals."

"So alignment does not mean," Al asked in clarification, "that I have to give up my desire to sell my portion of the business, and Robert does not have to give up his desire to pass his portion to his daughter? Sounds easier said than done."

"Yes, that's what I mean, and yes, it is easier said than done. It takes collaboration, cooperation, negotiation, and concessions. But it is possible and achievable.

"So, let's look at the Five Major Exit Goals," James continued. He noted with satisfaction that Al and Robert resumed taking notes. "We call these 'major goals' because they are usually among the most important goals to an owner contemplating exit, and because they have the greatest potential to cause incompatibility among co-owners. The Five Major Exit Goals are your Exit Strategy, Exit Timing, Exit Amount, Legacy, and Transition. Let me briefly explain each. Remember, I am going to give you a copy of 'The Guide to Creating Co-Owner Exit Alignment,' which will cover this information in more detail.

"The first major goal is your Exit Strategy. This means *how* you want to exit. There are only four exit strategies: pass your company to your family, sell to an outside buyer, sell to an inside buyer, or shut the company down. You gentlemen are already experiencing how your different desired exit strategies are causing conflict.

"The second major goal is your Exit Timing. This means *when* you ideally want to exit. Some owners want to exit sooner, and some later. Again, you two appear to have incompatible goals on Exit Timing—Al wants to exit sooner, and Robert wants to exit at a later time.

"The third major goal is Exit Amount. This means *how much* you want to exit for, in the financial sense. It is common that one co-owner is able and willing to exit for his or her proportionate share of the company's current total value, while another co-owner is either unable or unwilling to exit for his or her proportionate share of that same total value."

"We are zero for three so far," Al interrupted. "The amount I want to sell for, Robert says he could not afford to take."

"So it would seem," James responded. "Don't feel badly—that is not unusual. Rarely will you have two or more co-owners with personal financial situations so similar that they both are willing and able to exit for the same proportionate amount."

James paused for any comments or questions, and then continued. "The fourth major goal is Legacy. This means *in what condition* and *to whom* you want to leave your company. We have not discussed this today, beyond that Robert wants his daughter to have ownership one day. Examples of common Legacy goals include making sure valued employees are treated well during and after your exit, taking steps to protect and preserve the company's culture, or seeing that the company's reputation continues forward in a positive manner."

"How would co-owners disagree about that stuff, James?" Al asked. "I mean, what business owner is going to be against treating employees well or protecting the company's culture?"

"It's not so much that somebody would be against those things," James said, "but rather two or more co-owners could have different ideas on how to best achieve them and what priority to assign them. For example, one co-owner might want to share ownership with key employees to incent and thank them for their contribution, whereas another co-owner may not. Or in another example, one co-owner may want to sell the business to a certain buyer, but the other co-owner may perceive that that same potential buyer would be a poor culture fit and therefore object to selling the business to that particular buyer.

"The fifth and final major goal is Transition. This means *how involved* an owner wants to be during and after exit and how *control* is to be handled.

We have not discussed this either today. Some owners prefer to make a quick transition to leave and pursue other interests, while other owners prefer to remain involved with the company in some ongoing, perhaps limited capacity. Also, co-owners can have strong feelings about how control is to be addressed during transition, especially in situations where the business is being passed to the next family generation or sold to an internal buyer such as a co-owner or key employee. Business co-owners with incompatible exit goals in this area can find themselves unable to exit successfully until they find a way to create alignment.

"Those are the Five Major Exit Goals that co-owners need to gain alignment around in order to successfully exit. More often than not, business co-owners will have one or more goals within these five that are incompatible with each other's."

"It appears we are not in alignment on at least the first three, and perhaps even parts of four and five," Al observed pessimistically.

"I would need more time to discern where you are in alignment and not, and normally I'd meet with both of you one-on-one as part of that process," James responded. "I agree, however, that you have several exit goals which appear to be incompatible at this time."

"Where do we go from here?" Robert asked.

"Sure—you beat me to it," James replied with a smile. "Let me wrap up with a quick summary of the Seven Steps to Co-Owner Alignment. These too will be summarized in the follow-up guide that I will provide to you. The seven steps are—" Pausing, James began to quickly write on a piece of paper, then slid the sheet over for Al and Robert to assess. The list written on the paper read:

1. *Understand the issue*
2. *Establish who is involved*
3. *Determine preliminary exit goals*
4. *Share goals and identify incompatibilities*
5. *Eliminate Alignment Inhibitors*
6. *Implement Alignment Cultivators*
7. *Monitor and adjust with time*

"The first step is to understand the issues. I believe we've accomplished much of that today. You gentlemen seem to understand why co-owners face incompatible goals at exit, and why it's important.

"The second step is to establish who is involved. By default, we've already covered this step as well. You may not have exactly equal ownership within your company, but you openly refer to each other as equal partners in your approach to this business. That tells me you both intend to have a full say and equal decision-making authority.

"Your situation is not universal, however. There are other co-owner situations where some co-owners may be less involved in the exit-planning process. Imagine for a moment you both agreed to sell a very small portion of your business to a key employee. Once that key employee became an owner, he would have certain rights as an owner, but he likely would have less say in what happens than you because he owns a much smaller percentage and is brand new. There are a variety of reasons why some co-owners may have more input in the exit-planning process than others beyond just percentage of ownership. You can read more about that later in The Guide, if you wish."

"We are good on number two, James," Robert replied. "We are equal partners in this."

"The third step in creating co-owner alignment is for every co-owner involved in the process to determine his or her preliminary individual exit goals. It's impossible to know if we have goal compatibility or not if we don't know what our goals are. As you may have deduced, the Five Major Exit Goals are the most important goals for each co-owner to determine for him or herself.

"The fourth step, then, is for the co-owners to come together and share their individual goals so that we can identify areas of incompatibility and begin to create co-owner alignment. This can be a difficult step for co-owners for the reasons we talked about, which is why most co-owners get help from independent advisors. Yet it's a critical step. It's where the rubber will meet the road, so to speak."

"Hopefully without leaving skid marks all over everybody," Robert replied humorously. James laughed, but Al had a sullen look.

"The fifth step is to address and eliminate any Alignment Inhibitors which may exist. We already discussed a few examples, but there are more. Some of the Inhibitors can be harder to eliminate than others. The fewer Inhibitors that remain, the better.

"The sixth step is to implement what we call Alignment Creators. We did not talk about these today. Obviously, they are the opposite of Alignment Inhibitors. There are about two dozen commonly used mechanisms that provide a variety of means to help create co-owner alignment.

"Finally, the seventh step is to monitor and adjust with time. Things change with time, and nothing stays the same. As one or more co-owners get closer to exit, typically there is more work that needs to be done to exit successfully. Co-owners must frequently evaluate their progress and stay alert for changes in the marketplace, within the company, or within the co-owners themselves that could require the need to revisit and possibly revise the original plan."

"Is that all?" Al asked in a disheartened tone.

"Well," James replied, "admittedly, it probably seems like a lot at this point. Right now, you're at the beginning of the process and at a standstill. When you have zero momentum, gaining even a little speed takes a lot of effort. Once you get underway, these issues can become less daunting."

James checked his phone's screen and noted that it was time to conclude. "Gentlemen, I will e-mail you a copy of 'The Guide to Creating Co-Owner Exit Alignment' as a resource to follow up this conversation. Of course, if you would like to learn about our services helping co-owners like you, I would be honored to sit back down together. Otherwise, thank you for your time."

With that, Robert stood up, followed closely by James. Robert walked to him, shook his hand warmly, and said, "Thanks for today, James. I learned a lot, and I look forward to reading The Guide to help us." Robert then left the room without even acknowledging Al.

Al stood slowly and held his notepad with two hands, preventing any attempt from James to shake his hand. James thus remained standing and facing Al, unsure what might happen next.

"What did you and Robert talk about when I was out of the room?" Al asked accusingly.

"During the break?"

"Yes."

"Not much. We talked a little about his frustrations with all of this. We also talked about his daughter and her success here. Why?"

Al did not answer, but rather remained standing, examining him. James reminded himself that he could not help these two co-owners by being coy with them. "Al, you contacted me and asked me to sit down with you and Robert today. Did you get what you wanted from this meeting?"

"No. If you really want to know, I got the opposite."

"How so?"

"The numbers Taylor gave us are strong—very strong. Mergers and acquisitions activity in our industry is hot right now, and we'd be crazy to not sell as soon as possible. A year or two from now, prices could fall significantly. I expected you to talk some sense into Robert. Instead, all we got from you was business plans, job descriptions, and dizzying lists of goals for this and steps for that. Robert probably left here happy because everything you talked about would take years to implement. He probably thinks nobody is going anywhere anytime soon. That's not the case. I am going to sell. I have invested years of sacrifice and hard work into this company. I have the right to move on and do other things. It's not fair to my family if I don't get the maximum value from this business. As soon as possible I am selling my portion to whoever pays me a full price in cash."

When certain Al was done, James spoke. "Al, can we sit for just a minute? Please?"

Al slowly sat back down. James rejoined him at the table.

"First, I understand that you feel frustrated. Other business co-owners whom I have worked with felt that way too at the start of this process, but they found that the effort to address these issues pays off in the end, financially and otherwise. You said that to implement all of the things we talked about here would take years of work. I agree with you. To exit successfully usually takes years of preparation. Most business owners wait too long to get started. I often have to explain to owners that if they want to exit anytime within the next five years or sooner, then they have already entered the final stretch of the race, and it's time to start sprinting.

"All of that does not mean you have to be here for years to come. It also doesn't mean that you can't sell. If you want to sell your interest in the business sometime soon, then you and Robert may have to do the best you can with the limited time available. It seems pretty clear that Robert buying you out is an option. If you dig your heels in and insist on getting all cash at sale from him, then you two are probably stuck. If Robert refuses to take on at least some risk to buy you out, then you two are probably stuck. But if you compromise, perhaps together we can come up with a plan that meets your needs now and his needs later. I am certain that you two have compromised many times over the last seventeen years to make your relationship work. That doesn't change now that you're close to exiting. If anything, the need for compromise increases."

"I don't need a lecture, James," Al said testily.

"Forgive me," James said, holding his hand to his chest. "My wife and kids have told me once or twice that sometimes I come across that way."

James paused, and then asked, "Can I stop worrying for a moment about how I sound and just speak with you directly and bluntly?"

"Best question you asked me all day."

"Great. Thanks. Let's go back to the market-value estimates Taylor gave you. You said the numbers were strong. Could you have grown the company to that much value all by yourself?"

"You mean without Robert?"

James nodded.

"No way. I am not sure the company would have even survived without him. I'd like to think that he would say the same thing about me too. He and I have been a great team."

"Okay, so your one plus his one added up to three."

Al smiled. "Good way to put it."

"Sounds like you two accomplished something pretty special here. Now, you are wrapping up your run at Ark Technology Solutions. Having a co-owner requires you to do some extra work in preparation for exit. You have to take some extra steps, make some extra accommodations, and consider some extra concessions.

"What's in it for you to make this extra effort? Look again at the market-value estimate that the investment banker gave you. There's many millions of dollars in that number. From what you just told me, quite a few of those millions simply would not exist if you and Robert had not partnered together for these last seventeen years. True?"

"True . . ." Al said slowly.

"If you and he work together to align your exit plans, then the financial return on investment of doing this extra work is many millions of dollars more than you would have had, had you gone it alone. Right? If instead you dig your heels in and say, 'I want all of my money in cash right up front,' then you may not get it. Bluntly, you seem to be demanding something from Robert that you would not have if not for Robert.

"That's just the financial piece of the picture. If you and your partner can find a way to align your exit plans, then you also will create for yourself the peace of mind that comes from knowing you left behind a company positioned for continued success, led by good people who apply values consistent with your own.

"By the way, to be balanced, I can say the same things about Robert too. He can't have everything he wants either. There's quite a few millions in that number that he would not potentially have if not for you. Maybe more importantly to him, this business that he is excited to share with his daughter would not be all that it is if not for you."

Al lowered his eyes. The only noise in the room was the low hum of the building air-conditioning system. James counted to ten to force himself to not speak. Then fifteen. At nineteen he was about give in when—

"If he and I do this right, it will be a pretty good return on our investment, won't it?" Al finally asked, his eyes rising to meet James's.

"Yes, it will be."

"I just don't want to mess things up," Al said, rubbing his forehead with his fingertips. "We only have one shot at success here. I messed this up once already."

James did not understand what Al meant by his last comment, but he sensed asking would have to wait. "Well then, we have to make sure we do things right this time," James replied.

Al sat with his hands at his temples for another moment before finally standing. James joined him and the two men quietly shook hands. Al silently escorted James out of the conference room and down the hallway toward Ark's office lobby. As they reached the main door, James opened the door for himself and was about to say goodbye when Al put his hand on James's arm to stop him.

"You have given me a lot to think about, James. I have to admit that I don't really see how Robert and I are going to resolve these matters. We are barely speaking to each other at this point, as I am sure you noticed. But we have to try, I guess."

Al suddenly looked sad, almost remorseful. "Before Robert and I can work on our situation, you've made me realize there's something else that I need to do first." With that, Al let him pass and closed the door behind him.

James stood for a moment looking at the closed office door, wondering what Al meant.

Thursday, about 6:00 p.m.,
in Al's office at Ark Technology Solutions Inc.

Al sat at his desk, so intensely studying a line-of-credit term sheet from their bank that he failed to hear the knocking at his doorway. He was already working later than he wanted to this evening, for these documents had to be completed by tomorrow. A second round of knocks, louder than the first, broke through his concentration. He looked up to see Jessica standing in his open doorway, her fist hovering in the air next to the doorframe in case a third round would be needed. Seeing her, he lowered the bank documents and welcomed her in with a wave of his spare hand.

As Jessica entered, he noticed not for the first time how complete of a person she was. He had known her since before she was even a teenager, and she had grown into a smart, successful, driven person. Now she stood before him, formally standing in front of his desk despite two open armchairs available immediately before her.

"Hey Jessica, what can I do for you?" Al asked, hoping it would be brief. He wanted to finish reviewing the bank documents and get home.

"Thanks, Al," she opened. "Actually, I would like to know what's bothering my dad so much. It's clear to me something is, and he won't tell me. I know it's work related."

"Oh?" Al asked, taking the bank papers into his hands in the hopes Jessica would notice them. "Perhaps you should talk to him."

"I tried, but he told me nothing was wrong. I called my stepmom, but she said something 'small at his office was bothering him.' Both she and my dad sometimes forget that 'at his office' means my company, too. I have been here for more than five years now. You'd think they would remember that."

Al chuckled. "I am sure that's frustrating, Jessica. Keep in mind that your dad has nearly thirty years with you as his daughter, and only about five as a coworker. Some parenting habits take a while to change."

"That may be, but something important is bothering him. I know it. I thought you might know what it is." Jessica's rigid posture suggested she was not going anywhere until she found out.

Al wanted to tell her that he didn't know what it was, or that she should best ask her father, or that he'd be glad to help but he had to finish reviewing these bank documents by tomorrow. He wanted to say any and all of those things, but he didn't. Maybe he saw in his partner's daughter something of his own daughters, or maybe he just decided to be kind. Either way, to his surprise, he put the bank papers down and motioned for her to sit at one of the two small couches located on the far side of his expansive office. At first she resisted, but upon seeing his "you asked" look, she took a seat.

"I will be right back," he said to her confused look.

A minute later, Al returned and closed his office door behind him. He crossed the room and sat in the second couch, arranged catercorner to Jessica's. He handed her a cold can of beer, keeping a second for himself. Not waiting for Jessica, he popped open his beer to a satisfying *itshhh* sound and took a sip.

126

Jessica didn't have to ask Al where it came from. A six-pack sat buried in the back of the refrigerator in the employee break room, left over from an impromptu company happy hour months ago. She saw the beers peeking over someone's unclaimed yogurt cups every time she got something from the fridge. Not sure where this was going, Jessica decided to follow his lead and opened her beer as well.

"Do you know the story of how we named this company?" Al asked her.

"Ark?"

"Yes."

"I didn't know there was a story behind the name. I just assumed we liked the image—you know, the big boat protecting everybody. An important part of what we do is provide a safe haven for our clients."

"That is our logo, but it's not where the name came from. Well, at least not at first. We came up with 'Ark' by taking a letter from the names of the three company founders."

Jessica leaned forward. "There were only two founders," she said. Then, hesitantly, she added, "Weren't there?"

"No, there were three of us. The first letters of our first names were A, R, and K. From there we came up with the ark symbol and logo."

"I don't get it," Jessica replied. "A for Albert, of course. R for my father, Robert. Who is K? And how come I don't know any of this?"

"K founded the company with us, but after about a year the three of us had a falling-out. He left. We kept the name."

"Who was he?" Jessica sipped her beer, sitting transfixed on the edge of her seat.

"You know him. At least, you know of him."

"I do?" Jessica asked, perplexed. "Was he some distant uncle of mine or something? Come on, Al, who was K?"

"K stood for Kevin, as in Kevin Davidoff."

"What? You're kidding me!" Jessica leapt half out of her seat and spilled a small portion of beer on her hand. "Kevin Davidoff—as in the owner and founder of our biggest, nastiest competitor? He used to be your partner? My dad's partner? Okay, Al. This I gotta hear." Unconsciously wiping her hand dry on her jeans, she leaned back into the couch, anticipating that Al was about to tell her a story. She was right.

"As I said, this company was founded by three of us: your dad, Kevin Davidoff, and me. We all knew each other from working together at a prior company. While there, your father and I became friends and often talked about starting our own business. Things fell into place when

Kevin was hired to our department. He was a bright young talent. We liked him right away. One day after work—and after a lot of beer—the three of us decided to strike out on our own. Thus, Ark was born."

"That must have been exciting. I love hearing the stories about how new businesses are created."

"It was exciting. It was also scary. Launching Ark was a risk, especially for me and your dad. At the time I had two kids in school and a mortgage. Your dad had you, plus Ashley, and another one on the way."

"My other half sister, Elizabeth."

"Right. Elizabeth. Kevin was, now that I think about it, about your age at the time. He had a girlfriend and lived in an apartment, so he did not have any of the overhead that your father and I had. Either way, it was a risk.

"But the risk paid off. We managed to land two big accounts right away, and then several more. Against the odds, within just a few months we were making money. At first we worked out of my house, as you may have heard. The three of us wedged into my den for an office. Later, when we hired our first employees, they worked out of my basement. It was cramped, and we probably violated a zoning ordinance somewhere along the way, but it worked."

"How did Valerie deal with all of that?" Jessica asked, trying to picture Al's wife with her house full of fresh young Ark employees.

"She was great, as she always is," Al said with fondness. "She insisted on feeding everybody dinner if they were still working past six, as many days we were. We were covered up with work. It was fun. Robert and Kevin were great to work with. It was exciting, as you said.

"Working from my house would not last, however. Eventually we moved into a small office we subleased for a cheap rate. By the end of our first year, we had about a dozen employees including the three of us, and more work than we could handle. We also had cash in the bank. That's when the problems started."

"Really? How does cash create problems?" Jessica asked.

It was then that Al realized he made the right decision in telling his business partner's daughter this story. She needed to know it. He continued, "Cash can cause just as many problems among co-owners as a lack of cash. I had two kids in college. Your dad had a young and growing family. I needed to take some of that cash home to pay some bills, and your dad felt the same way. We got off to such a good start that the three of us had managed to pay ourselves a modest salary almost from the beginning, but it was still less than your dad and I had been making before starting the company. I wanted to take home some of our profits, as did your dad. Kevin did not. He was young and hungry. He wanted us to reinvest every dollar back into the business. He thought that given how fast our new business was already growing, if we pressed the gas pedal all the way down we could grow twice as fast."

"How much are we talking about, Al?" Jessica asked.

"By then we had somewhere around a hundred thousand dollars of cash on hand that we had no immediate need for. Split three ways, we could each take thirty-three thousand home. Not a huge amount, but Robert and I could have paid a lot of bills with it. But, it also was enough money that if we had reinvested it back into business, we could have hired more people and accelerated our growth. Kevin was right about that."

"What happened?" Jessica asked, not aware the beer can in her hand was now empty.

"Robert and I started talking about taking this money out of the business. Your dad shared with me that he and Tess could use the extra money at home. I told him the same was true for Valerie and me."

"Where was Kevin during these conversations?"

Al winced, then answered, "At first, we didn't directly ask Kevin what he wanted to do. I told myself at the time 'Who objects to getting thirty-three thousand dollars?' I was sure Kevin would agree. I realize now that was only an excuse. I now see that your dad and I didn't initially include Kevin in those conversations because he was younger than we were, and we probably were not regarding him as an equal partner. Plus, I was CEO, and Robert and I were two-thirds of the ownership. Deep down, I felt like I didn't need Kevin's permission to distribute any profits. Legally I was right, but what a business co-owner can do that is legally right is sometimes different from what a business co-owner should do that is right for the relationship.

"Things might have been okay had Robert and I talked with Kevin upfront and told him of our intentions. We were going to talk to him of course; I wasn't just going to send him a check for thirty-three thousand without any conversation. But before we could tell him, Kevin came in one day and asked to meet with your dad and me about an important matter. He seemed serious, so we dropped everything and sat down together. To our surprise, Kevin put in front of us an expansion plan showing how we could open a second office and double in size over the next twelve to eighteen months. He clearly had worked hard on his plan—I remember it was more than a dozen pages of carefully written notes. We spent over two hours talking about his plan. His ideas were good. It likely would have worked. But, his plan required us to reinvest all of that surplus cash, plus our future profits for the next one to two years. It was too much risk for me—and your father.

"At the end of this meeting, I broke the news to Kevin that your father and I already were discussing the surplus cash. I explained that we needed to take our share out of the business to provide for our families. I could see the rejection on Kevin's face. Your dad pointed out that we still were enjoying excellent growth, and Kevin's expansion plan could be implemented at some later point. I pointed out some of Kevin's ideas which we could implement now, because they could be funded out of current earnings. However, opening a second office and expanding at the rate he proposed was not going to happen, at least not at that point in time."

"How did he take this?"

"Fine, or so I thought. Kevin said he understood, thanked us for the meeting, and took back his handwritten notes. I thought we had let Kevin down gently and we would all move forward together. I was wrong. I was wrong about how Kevin felt, and both your dad and I were wrong in what we did."

"Wrong? What did you and my father do that was wrong?" Jessica interjected.

"Robert and I were wrong to decide we would take money out of the business without first having a discussion among the three of us. What to do with surplus profits is probably an ownership-level decision, as I only recently learned. All of the owners should have had the opportunity to offer input before a decision was made. Your dad and I made our decisions before Kevin even had a chance. That was not fair to him. Robert and I still might have made the same decision—I am pretty sure we would have. But Kevin never had any input, and so he didn't support the decision. People won't buy in if they don't have a chance to weigh in.

"Unfortunately, I also know now that we made some other mistakes too—all three of us. For example, we did not have anything in the way of a business plan. We started Ark based on a dozen beers and a whim, backed up by a few key customers that we thought would come with us if we went out on our own. The customers came, which was great. But we did not have any kind of plan saying where we were going and how we were going to get there. Robert, Kevin, and I never discussed in advance any of the what-ifs, such as 'What if we can't make payroll?' or 'What if we get an offer to sell the company?' or—"

"What if you have more money in the bank than you expected? What would you do with it?" Jessica interrupted, unable to stay silent any longer.

"Right," Al replied thoughtfully. "When co-owners have no shared plan for everyone to follow, and one day there's more money in the bank than you expected to have, a funny thing happens. Every owner gets his or her own ideas about what should happen to that money. Nobody is wrong, mind you, but nobody is completely right either. Kevin's ideas were good. My and your dad's idea was fine too, but just different. Worse than different—our ideas were incompatible. When co-owners are not working from a common business plan, then at every important question they fall into the trap of making decisions based on who feels most strongly, or lobbies the hardest, or has the most assertive personality. That's no way to run a business."

"Why not just split the money in half?" Jessica asked.

"In hindsight that could have worked if we talked it through earlier and together. But Kevin allocated all of the money in his mind for his expansion plan. In our minds, your dad and I allocated all of the money to take home. By the time we finally talked about it together, each of us was already set in his own mind. Besides, we never had the chance to compromise. I thought Kevin was fine with our decision. When I finally learned he wasn't, it was too late."

"Why? When did Kevin leave?" Jessica asked.

"The day after he got his thirty-three-thousand-dollar check."

"You're kidding."

"Nope. He never said anything to us. No goodbye, no resignation letter, nothing. At first we didn't know what happened to him. He did not return any calls to his apartment. For a day or so we worried he might be injured or missing. Finally, I reached his girlfriend. She's the one who told us that he quit. He just never bothered to tell us."

"That's cold," Jessica said, trying to picture the scene.

"Probably. He could have handled things a bit better. He was angry. Anyway, within a week after leaving us, Kevin established The Davidoff Company. He immediately began going after our customers. He contacted all of them and tried to lure them away, often undercutting us on price by large amounts. He succeeded, too. Many of our customers went with his new company, including some of our biggest and best. Of the customers we managed to keep, in many cases we had to cut our pricing to fend him off, further increasing our financial losses.

"He had most of the advantages over us—it often works that way when a partner or top employee leaves to become your competition. He knew all our customers and current prospects. He knew all our strengths and weaknesses. Making things worse, we were spending so much time fighting to keep our current customers that new sales tanked. Our revenues fell further. Cash dried up. Soon we had to lay off employees. Your dad and I were forced to put back into the company the thirty-three thousand dollars we each had taken out. I have to tell you, that was a low point in my marriage. My wife was not happy. I am sure your stepmom was not pleased either. I felt like I failed my family. The extra cash helped hold things together, but only barely. By the time we hit bottom, we were down to four employees, two of whom were your dad and me."

"What about a noncompete? How could Kevin just take those customers with him?" Jessica asked, trying to imagine how stressful this must have been for Al and Robert.

"That's a good question. When we first started hiring people, we worked with a lawyer who created for us a standard agreement for employees to sign. It included noncompete and nonsolicitation language, as much as the state allows, in my understanding. But you know what? The three of us never made ourselves sign it. I know this sounds crazy, but we thought of ourselves as owners, not employees, so we exempted ourselves. Dumb, I know. Business co-owners can't operate outside the normal employee practices and procedures used to protect the business just because they are owners."

"Did you consider suing him?"

"We talked about it, but there wasn't any money to be spent on the process. Instead, we reached out to Kevin to resolve things by buying him out. He replied via registered mail and asked for some ridiculous amount for his stake, an amount he knew we would never pay. I now understand that he felt like we ganged up on him. He thought that it would always be two against one in major business decisions, and he would always be outvoted. He assumed that Robert and I would do this to him all the time—talk about things without him and let him know our decisions after the fact. I don't believe Robert and I would have done that to him, but we did it to him once, didn't we? I can't really blame Kevin for feeling as though he could not trust us."

"How could you know that's how Kevin was feeling?" Jessica asked doubtfully.

"Because he told me at lunch today," Al replied, expecting to see shock on Jessica's face. He was not disappointed.

"What?" she asked. "Wait, wait—don't say another word, Al. I need another beer . . . and so do you."

132

Al only had to wait a moment before she returned with two more cold cans of beer. She passed one to him before sitting back down. "Okay, I want to hear all about lunch, but first go back to when he was competing with you and my dad."

"He still competes with us, Jessica," Al pointed out, a tinge of bitterness in his voice. Seeing her look of recognition, Al continued. "After a while, the dust settled. Any customer that Kevin would be able to lure away had already left. We began to claw our way back. The anger faded, and about a year later, through our respective lawyers, we reached an agreement to buy his interest in the company."

Seeing the question on her face, Al volunteered, "The buyout amount was twenty-five thousand. Ark was not worth much after all the losses. Kevin agreed to let us pay him over seven years, so the payments were only a few hundred bucks per month. I think everybody just wanted to move on. From there, Kevin went his way, and your dad and I went ours. Less than two years into the buyout, we scrounged together enough cash to pay off the remaining balance we owed him. Robert and I did not like writing checks to him each month. It put a bad taste in our mouths every thirty days."

Jessica paused, absorbing the story. "Wow, I never knew any of this. The Davidoff Company is big—several times our size. Kevin Davidoff has an amazing reputation. I heard him speak once at a local technology association event. He's a real visionary. A good-looking guy too, if you don't mind me saying," Jessica said with a wry smile.

"Al, have you ever thought about how things might have turned out if you three stayed together? I mean, his company and ours are two of the larger players in the market. Together, we could have dominated. Am I a jerk for pointing that out?" Jessica focused on Al's face to gauge his reaction.

"No, you are not a jerk. I don't think about Kevin very often—at least not any more. When I do, I'll admit to asking myself the same question. The missed opportunities are really the biggest cost when business co-owners do not get along. It's not the money we spent and lost competing, nor the legal bills, nor even the buyout money. The biggest cost was the business growth we did not achieve because we did not have compatible goals, because we were rowing in different directions. Even once we realized that we were not in alignment, we did not work hard enough to get back on the same page. We didn't know how to. I also learned just recently that we committed a number of mistakes that made getting and staying in alignment harder than it otherwise might have been.

"I suspect that had the three of us stayed together, today we'd have an even bigger and more profitable company. Even if we later split up over another issue, we could have avoided losing all that time and going through all of that stress if we had handled things differently. We ruined a good working relationship. We also caused some people to lose their jobs along the way, employees who had no fault in all of this. It's not a story that I like to tell, Jessica—the story of how we did it wrong."

"Is that why nobody around here knows any of this?" she inquired.

"I guess. After Kevin left, Robert and I told the employees to never say his name aloud. At first we did this out of spite and anger. Later, I just wanted to start fresh, to have a clean story for the organization. Most of our initial employees, the ones who knew Kevin, had to be let go during our freefall. The couple employees remaining who actually remembered him eventually left for various reasons. Once they were gone, Robert and I became the only ones who ever knew Kevin, and knew what A-R-K truly means."

His story over, Al took several swallows of his beer, as did Jessica. She tried to picture her dad putting money back into the company, struggling to keep a reeling business afloat and provide for a young family. She felt like she was learning something important about her dad that she never knew, in addition to something important about being a business owner. She also could not resist picturing in her mind Kevin Davidoff, about her age, feeling like his business partners cut him out. That must have hurt, too. Thinking about Kevin reminded her of something.

"I almost forgot about your lunch today. Do you meet with Kevin often?"

Al said nothing for a moment. After going this far, however, he knew he should finish. "Today was the first time Kevin Davidoff and I spoke since the day I handed him that thirty-three-thousand-dollar check more than fifteen years ago."

"What? You're joking."

"I assure you I am not."

"Wow. Why on earth did he call you after all this time?" Jessica could not stop her imagination from quickly supplying theories as to why Kevin would contact Al after all this time. Maybe The Davidoff Company was going to buy Ark?

"He didn't call me. I called him yesterday afternoon and invited him out to lunch. He told me he was free today. During lunch, I apologized."

"You did *what*?" Jessica exclaimed, half jumping off the couch again. "Apologized for what? I heard what you did wrong, Al. You talked about the surplus cash without him, and you guys didn't have a business plan. But what you guys did to Kevin was nothing compared to what Kevin did to you, to this company. He stole your customers—our customers. He almost made us go under from the sound of it. What do you have to apologize for? If anything, he should be apologizing to you and to my father." Jessica's face flushed from the combination of beer and anger.

"Jessica, I appreciate what you are saying. Kevin does carry some blame in what happened. But I still needed to apologize. Whether you think my mistakes were bigger or smaller than his, I still made mistakes. I recently realized this. I needed to see him to apologize, for me. I wanted to tell him that I was sorry for cutting him out and giving him reason to believe he could not trust me or your dad. I also told him that I was glad for his business success since leaving us, and respected all that he had achieved at his company."

"That's crazy stuff, Al—forgive me, but it is. Geez. What did he do? Choke on his cheeseburger?"

Al laughed. "There was never a need during our meal for the Heimlich maneuver, but I'm pretty sure he was caught off guard. I suspect he thought I was up to something. After a while, I believe he saw I had no ulterior motive. Once we got to that point, he said he appreciated me coming to him. If it makes you feel better, Jessica, he also apologized to me. He said he regretted quitting Ark like he did and going after our customers. He admitted that he had to cut prices so low to get most of them to switch that he lost money on those accounts for years. We both laughed at that. He said he was 'young and hot' back then—"

Jessica arched an eyebrow.

"I am pretty sure he was referring to his temper, not his looks."

"Gotcha."

"Anyway," Al continued, "he admitted to overreacting all those years ago. He also talked about how owning a business has helped him learn patience and humility. When lunch was over he must have thanked me four or more times for calling him. My lunch with Kevin was one of the best business experiences I've ever had, Jessica."

"That's incredible, Al. Did you tell my father all of this?" Jessica asked. "What did he say?"

"I didn't have to. Before I could get back to the office after lunch, your father called me. He said, 'Guess who I just spoke with?' It turns out Kevin called him immediately after leaving the restaurant, told him of our lunch, and made the same apology to your father that he made to me. Robert was in shock, as you can imagine.

"That got your dad and me talking. We had a good conversation—our first in a long time. I even pulled over on the side of the road so that I wasn't driving while on the phone with him. We spoke about our relationship, and some of the things we need to figure out together."

Jessica fell quiet, reflecting for a moment before continuing. "Al, that's a pretty amazing thing you did, apologizing to him out of the blue. Why did you do it? And why are you telling me all of this? I know you well enough to know that you are not bragging about taking the high road."

"I am still figuring out a few things for myself. I know enough to tell you that recently I have been repeating some of the mistakes I made with Kevin, only this time with your father. I needed to make things right with Kevin in order to make sure I get things right this time with Robert. I am telling you this so that you can learn from me—from us. One day you might co-own a business—perhaps this business. You cannot avoid the mistakes we made as business owners unless you know about them in the first place," Al said quietly.

"What mistakes were you repeating?" Jessica asked, her eyes gentle.

"Quite a few I am afraid, mostly dealing with co-owners needing to work together. I told you about Kevin because I see now what happens if co-owners don't do things the right away. With your father, I've done some things the wrong way again. Robert and I need to work on our exit goals and figure out how to compromise so that our future plans can be in alignment. It's not going to be easy, but I believe it will be worth the effort. Plus, we'll have some help this time. Your father and I recently received a document which guides business co-owners through the process of creating alignment around their exit goals. Once we both read it, we intend to . . ."

As Jessica listened, she found herself admiring Al for his candor and willingness to admit his mistakes and learn from them. A deep sense of gratitude blanketed her, not just for the chance to work at such a forward-moving business as Ark, but for working with two leaders whom she so deeply respected.

THE END

To: *Beaman, Al; Gilmore, Robert*
From: *Rigney, James*
Message: *Follow-up to meeting / The Guide*

Al and Robert,

Thank you for the opportunity to meet yesterday.

As per our conversation, please find attached a copy of "The Guide to Creating Co-Owner Exit Alignment." This resource explores why exit-goal incompatibility among business co-owners commonly occurs, explains the importance of creating co-owner exit alignment, and presents a step-by-step process for co-owners to follow to create exit alignment.

Please contact me if you have any immediate questions. Otherwise I will follow up with you shortly.

Sincerely,

James Rigney

The Guide to Creating Co-Owner Exit Alignment

I

Introduction

Growing and leading your business up to this point is probably one of your life's greatest achievements. While business success can bring about satisfying personal wealth, for most owners it is not just about money. A sense of deep fulfillment comes from building something from the ground up, creating jobs, delivering quality products and services, and providing for loved ones. Your achievement is that much more cherished for the fact that your business experienced success while so many others failed. If building and growing a closely held business were easy, more people would do it.

A successful exit is the capstone on your business successes. It's the opportunity to reach financial independence, create the freedom to do what you want when you want, and usher forward a sustainable, well-led business that upholds your values and standards.

If you share ownership in your business with other business co-owners, then ultimately your ability to successfully exit is likely tied to their own ability to do the same. Your exit goals could undermine theirs, or the reverse. Put two or more co-owners together, and it is almost inevitable that they will have different exit goals. Perhaps one co-owner wants to exit sooner, another wants to exit later. One may want to sell the business, another wants to pass it down to his or her children. One needs more money at exit to be happy, another needs less. One wants a quick exit, another wants to stay with the company for the longer term. Yet no matter the differences, it's vital to understand that no one is right or wrong in these situations; the co-owners just have different goals. Additionally, as the number of owners increases, the likelihood that the co-owners have different goals increases to a near certainty.

Goal incompatibility at exit comes in degrees. Some business co-owners have exit goals which are only partially or marginally conflicting. Others have exit goals which are fully and completely incompatible. Regardless of the degree and depth of their goal incompatibility, undesirable things can happen. Goal incompatibility, if left unaddressed, can at a minimum cause stress, strained relationships, stunted business growth, increased legal and operating risks, and more expensive and difficult exits. When goal incompatibility at exit is at its worst, it often leads to deep anguish or guilt, broken relationships, millions in lost business value, legal confrontations, and outright failed exits.

Consequently, business co-owners must address exit-goal incompatibility when encountered and ultimately create alignment around their important exit goals. It's important to realize that alignment does not mean having identical goals, as it's common for co-owners to have different exit plans. Alignment means the co-owners' individual goals are calibrated to be in sync, meaning one co-owner's goals will not interfere with or outright derail another co-owner's exit success. Without alignment, you and your co-owners may find yourselves rowing your mutually owned boat in different directions.

How to Use this Guide

This Guide is intended to provide business co-owners and their advisors with ideas and strategies on how to create alignment around co-owners' exit goals. Because exit planning involves a range of tax, legal, financial, business, and personal issues, co-owners must seek advice from advisors experienced in these issues. The most important advisors are an exit planner, accountant, and attorney. Other advisors that may play an important role, depending on the co-owners' exit goals, could include a mergers and acquisitions (M&A) advisor, commercial banker, investment advisor, and/or business coach.[*]

---

[*] For more information about the advisory team, please reference *Dance in the End Zone: The Business Owner's Exit Planning Playbook*. Patrick A. Ungashick. Alpharetta, GA: BookLogix, 2013.

This Guide addresses the exit goals, needs, and challenges that co-owners of a business commonly face. However, every business and every owner is unique. Therefore, there is no perfect recipe on how to create exit alignment for co-owners; it would not even be possible to assemble a definitive cookbook which includes all the possible recipes. Ultimately, co-owners and their advisors will need to create customized solutions which address the specific goals and challenges facing that business and its co-owners.

II

Why Must Business Co-Owners Collaborate on Their Exit Plans? (The Three-Link Chain)

The connection between being a business co-owner and the need for co-owners to create alignment at exit can be understood by imagining a chain with three links upon which a sentence is printed. This conceptual tool is called the Three-Link Chain. The first link says:

> *Business owners cannot achieve*
> *their major goals without a successful exit.*

Business owners usually share a similar set of desired outcomes for their exit. These most commonly include reaching financial security, having the freedom to do what you want to do, and creating a sustainable business legacy. For most owners, all of these desired outcomes are only realized with a successful business exit. To reach financial freedom, most owners need to unlock the majority of their wealth which is tied up in their business and its supporting assets. To have the freedom to do what you want to do, most owners need to turn the business over to new ownership and leadership. To create a sustainable business legacy, most owners need to successfully exit and demonstrate that the business cannot only survive without them, but actually thrive.

The second link in the chain says:

> *Business co-owners cannot successfully*
> *exit if their goals are incompatible with one another.*

When a business has two or more co-owners, some or all of the co-owners cannot successfully exit if their individual goals are incompatible with one another. It is common that one owner's goals will hinder, disrupt, or outright block one or more of the other owners' goals. There are many ways this can occur. For example, one co-owner may want to sell the business to an outside buyer, whereas another co-owner wants to pass the business down to family. In other examples, the co-owners could have different exit time frames, or vastly different dollar amounts they want at exit, or conflicting beliefs on who should lead the business going forward. Sometimes the co-owners have goals which are only mildly conflicting. Sometimes the co-owners' goals appear to be completely irreconcilable.

The third link in the chain says:

> *Goal compatibility can only be achieved with*
> *a conscious and ongoing effort to create co-owner alignment.*

Goal incompatibility rarely goes away on its own. If anything, waiting makes matters worse because with less time, co-owners will have fewer solutions. Therefore, co-owners must proactively work to create and maintain an aligned approach to exit planning, working together collaboratively to implement strategies and tactics that enable every involved owner to successfully exit.

The Three-Link Chain illustrates the connection between business owners needing to successfully exit one day, and business co-owners needing to work together to make this happen.

III

Why Is Goal Incompatibility at Exit Practically Inevitable?

Some degree of goal incompatibility at exit is practically inevitable. It is helpful to understand this from the get-go because often co-owners and the people around them (close family members, employees, advisors, etc.) see the signs of co-owners struggling with exit-goal incompatibility and interpret it to be a relationship problem, which is not always the case. Goal incompatibility at exit has nothing to do with the quality or duration of the co-owners' relationships. (It is true, however, that co-owners who already are not getting along well will often experience deeper discord once they realize that their exit goals are in conflict.) Rather, exit-goal incompatibility is a natural, almost predictable event, rooted in the practically unavoidable differences between two or more people. Knowing this helps take some of the sting out of the issue and enables co-owners to address their needs more constructively and objectively.

No two business co-owners are exactly the same. Their biographical and situational differences plant the seeds which blossom into different goals at exit. The following table lists fifteen differences, each of which can lead to incompatible exit goals among business co-owners.

Table 1:

Co-Owner Differences That Can Cause Exit-Goal Incompatibility

Difference	How It Causes Exit-Goal Incompatibility
Ownership percentage	Disproportionate ownership often causes different financial challenges and opportunities at exit.
Age	Older co-owners often want to exit sooner and/or make a quicker exit transition.
Job position/responsibilities	Co-owners with more demanding and stressful positions may seek to exit sooner and/or make a quicker transition.
Income from the business	Co-owners receiving greater income from the business may be more financially dependent on the business, and therefore need more money at exit to reach financial freedom.
Outside income	Co-owners with greater income from sources outside the business may need less money from the business at exit to reach personal financial freedom.
Lifestyle costs	Co-owners with higher lifestyle costs may need more money at exit to reach financial freedom.
Family profile	Co-owners with larger families, extended families, or blended families may have higher lifestyle costs, and therefore need more money at exit to reach financial freedom and/or prefer to exit later in life.
Work/life balance desires	Co-owners who desire greater personal freedom may seek to exit sooner and/or with a quicker transition.
Other family members involved in the business	Co-owners who have one or more family members working in the business may seek to keep the business within family ownership rather than sell the business.
Method of becoming an owner	Co-owners who founded the business often have stronger legacy needs and goals compared to co-owners who came into ownership at a later date.

Table 1 Continued:
Co-Owner Differences That Can Cause Exit-Goal Incompatibility

Difference	How It Causes Exit-Goal Incompatibility
Outside interests and activities	Co-owners who are eager to pursue interests and activities outside of the business may seek to exit sooner and/or with a quicker transition.
Sense of self-identify	Co-owners whose sense of self-identity is rooted in their role within the business may wish to exit later in life and/or maintain an ongoing role with the business even after exit.
Risk tolerance	Co-owners with less tolerance for risk may seek to exit sooner and/or diversify their net worth away from a large concentration inside the business.
Health	Co-owners dealing with health challenges may seek to exit sooner to recuperate or pursue other life interests. Conversely, co-owners with known health issues may seek to maintain employment in the business to preserve medical insurance and other benefits.
Business ambitions	Co-owners who seek significant additional business growth and accomplishments may seek to exit later and/or make their exit conditional on achieving these outcomes.

This list is not exhaustive—co-owners could experience a variety of personal, cultural, or psychological differences that can contribute to different goals at exit. Furthermore, many co-owners are living examples of the "opposites attract" phenomenon. Their personality differences give their working relationship strength and effectiveness, but at exit those differences contribute to conflicting goals. Most business co-owners will have multiple differences between them, any one of which can lead to incompatible exit goals. As the number of co-owners increases, the number of differences usually increases exponentially. As a result, it should be easy to see why incompatible goals at exit occur so frequently and predictably.

IV

Why Does Business Success Often Increase Goal Incompatibility?

Ironically, successfully growing the business often increases the likelihood and degree of exit-goal incompatibility among co-owners. There are several reasons for this. First, as a business's revenue, profits, and surplus cash increase, different co-owners often develop different ideas about what to do with the increased financial resources. The greater the revenue, profits, and surplus cash, the greater the potential variety of ideas. For example, suppose a business has accumulated a significant amount of surplus cash. One co-owner may want to take it out of the business to increase his or her personal wealth, while another co-owner may want to reinvest that cash to accelerate business growth. Neither co-owner is right nor wrong. They just have different goals. Contrast that to a company that is small and not yet profitable. Its co-owners usually are in strong alignment with the goal of growing their company—the surplus profits simply do not exist.

The second reason why increased business success adds to the likelihood for incompatible exit goals has to do with the number of employees and the job specialization that ensues. As most businesses grow, more people are employed, and those employees specialize. Contrast that with a very small business, such as a start-up. Its co-owners typically must be jacks-of-all-trades, taking turns doing anything and everything to grow the business. Later, once the business reaches a certain scale, it adds additional employees, allowing the co-owners working in that business to specialize. As these co-owners specialize in a certain topic having to do with the business, they take on different roles and responsibilities. Some roles are more stressful, and some demand longer hours. Some roles are easier to replace at exit, and some are more difficult to transition and replace. These differences can contribute to the co-owners having different goals at exit. For example, some co-owners will be eager to exit or make a quicker transition. Other co-owners may be less eager to exit or may desire to remain with the company in some capacity even after exit. This is not preordained—every co-owner with a stressful role will not necessarily want a quick exit. Yet the differences in roles and responsibilities often influence different goals at exit.

The third and final way that business success contributes to exit-goal incompatibility is simply that the number of co-owners likely increases in direct relation to the business size. As a company gets bigger and older, it's typical for the number of co-owners to increase. It happens a variety of ways. Over time, families may pass ownership to siblings, children, cousins, or grandchildren. Or, investors attracted to the business's growth may buy into the business. Perhaps key employees receive ownership, either as an incentive or by purchasing into the business. The more successful the business, the more these opportunities for additional co-owners occur. As the number of co-owners increases, the potential for incompatible goals greatly increases simply because the homogeneity of the group decreases.

V

If Exit-Goal Incompatibility Is Common, Why Is It Not More Widely Acknowledged?

Most business co-owners face some degree of goal incompatibility at exit, yet the issue is not widely recognized nor addressed. To start, many co-owners will not discover they face goal incompatibility until they start preparing for exit. Many co-owners do not discuss exit in any detail until late in their relationship, when one or more co-owners have sufficiently aged and the need to address exit becomes acute. When co-owners do finally discuss exit, if they face goal incompatibility, unfortunately they often immediately cease any further discussion. Co-owners find these issues difficult to confront out of fear of damaging their relationship with one another. Also, once co-owners finally realize they face this issue, it is not a topic they readily want to admit to outsiders. Few co-owners would want their customers, employees, competitors, or peers to know these challenges are happening. Finally, exit often seems far enough in the future, and the company has enough immediate needs, that co-owners often (wrongly) conclude that dealing with their exit incompatibilities can wait for another day without causing harm.

Discovering late in the game that goal incompatibility exists, and/or putting off dealing with it, is not ideal. The sooner co-owners become aware of their incompatible exit goals and address the issues, the more options they have on how to create alignment. Co-owners who discover their incompatibilities shortly before exit (generally anything less than five years prior to exit), or put off dealing with it, will learn that creating alignment is far more difficult.

VI

What Are the Five Major Exit Goals around Which Co-Owners Need Alignment?

Most business owners have multiple goals they wish to achieve at exit. The most desired goal is financial freedom, which means working after exit is a personal choice and not a financial necessity. Other commonly held exit goals include controlling the timing and manner of one's exit, leaving behind a healthy and well-led business, preserving the company's culture, and having meaningful activities in one's life after exit.

Business co-owners need to create alignment around their individual exit goals in order to achieve collective success. Remember that aligned does not mean matching or identical. Different co-owners can have different exit goals, and this is usually the case. Alignment means one co-owner's goals cannot interfere with or undermine another co-owner's goals.

While it is possible to list dozens of potential goals that could be incompatible between two or more co-owners, there are Five Major Exit Goals that most owners pursue in their exit planning which have the greatest potential to be incompatible among business co-owners. In some situations, co-owners will find themselves with incompatible goals in only one or perhaps two of these Five Major Goals. In other situations, co-owners may find themselves with opposing goals in as many as four or all five areas. As one would expect, the more major goals in conflict, the more difficult creating alignment becomes.

Patrick A. Ungashick

The Five Major Exit Goals are:

1. Exit Strategy

The first major goal is Exit Strategy. This means *how* you want to exit. There are only four exit strategies: pass your business on to your family, sell to an outside buyer, sell to an inside buyer (one or more other co-owners and/or key employees), or shut down the company.* Co-owners with different and incompatible exit strategies often find themselves facing a seemingly irresolvable impasse. For example, one co-owner wants to pass the business down to his child, whereas another co-owner wants to sell the business to an outside buyer for the maximum value. Without breaking the company apart, these two co-owners appear to have incompatible exit strategies. Another common situation is a co-owner wants to sell his or her interest to one or more key employees, whereas another co-owner wants to pursue selling the business to outside buyers because they typically bring more cash and will potentially pay a higher price.

Gaining alignment for co-owners with incompatible Exit Strategy goals can be difficult because each of the four different exit strategies offers outcomes that the other three strategies usually cannot replicate. Passing one's business to family fulfills strong emotional desires that the other three exit strategies cannot meet. Selling the business to an outside buyer usually provides the maximum potential purchase price and cash at closing. Selling the business to an inside buyer can fulfill legacy aspirations the owner may have around rewarding partners or key employees. Creating alignment within this goal may require co-owners to consider switching their exit strategy, but only if alternative means are found to provide the outcomes that came with their original strategy.

2. Exit Timing

The second major goal is your Exit Timing. This means *when* you ideally want to exit. Some business owners are willing to be flexible on the timing of their exit, while others have strongly held aspirations in this area. For

---

* Occasionally some owners suggest that holding onto their business until death is a fifth exit strategy, presumably practiced to enjoy an income stream from the business along the way. This author's opinion is that death is not a strategy. Rather, it is a timing matter. At a business owner's death, one of these four outcomes still occurs: the business will pass to family, be sold to an outsider, be sold to an insider, or be shut down. For more information about the four exit strategies and how to determine which strategy is right for you, see *Dance in the End Zone: The Business Owner's Exit Planning Playbook*. Patrick A. Ungashick. Alpharetta, GA: BookLogix, 2013.

those owners, it is easy to see why controlling exit timing is important to them; no owner wants to leave his or her company before they are ready, and no owner wants to be required to stick around in a business when he or she has other interests to pursue. Also, exit timing is not as simple as targeting a date to cease being a business owner. Some owners prefer to phase down their ownership over time, selling (or giving to family) their ownership in batches, if possible.

Put two or more co-owners together, and it is common that they initially express exit timing goals that are incompatible. Some co-owners want to exit sooner, some later. Age is the dominant determinant. A co-owner in his sixties will more likely seek to exit sooner than a co-owner who is ten or twenty years younger. Other factors contributing to timing incompatibility include health, post-exit aspirations, business ambition, and work-life balance, as previously explored in this Guide.

On the surface, when co-owners have different exit-timing goals, the solution may seem as simple as compromising to split the difference. Sometimes this works. However, if the co-owners' desired exit timetables are off by many years or even a decade or more, meeting in the middle may be unacceptable for everyone.

3. Exit Amount

The third major goal is Exit Amount. This means *how much* money you aspire to have at exit to create financial freedom or fulfill other financial goals.* To most owners, reaching the Exit Amount goal is the highest priority. Rarely will a business owner voluntarily exit without achieving his financial goals. The challenge is that no two co-owners share identical financial circumstances. They will be different in a range of factors that influence their financial needs: family size, lifestyle costs, age, outside income sources, and other factors previously discussed in this Guide. Therefore, the norm is that co-owners have different exit-amount goals at exit, and sometimes the difference is so great as to be incompatible. In incompatible situations, one co-owner is able and willing to exit for his proportionate share of the company's total value, while another co-owner is either unable or unwilling to exit for his or her proportionate share of that same total value.

---

* See the author's white paper "Your Exit Magic Number™" to learn the special steps business owners need to take to calculate the net amount needed to reach financial freedom. Ungashick, Patrick. *The Exit Magic Number: The Most Important Number To A Business Owner*. NAVIX Consultants, 2015. Web.

Example: QRS Company had two equal co-owners, Co-Owner Senior (in his early sixties) and Co-Owner Junior (in his late forties). QRS's industry experienced a wave of acquisitions, and the two co-owners began to receive multiple offers to sell. Junior rejected all-cash purchase offers of first $10 million, then later $12 million, and finally $14 million. If Junior agreed to a sale at those prices, the after-tax net proceeds would have been insufficient to support his family's desired lifestyle, and he would be left approaching age fifty and facing the choice of either working for somebody else or starting a completely new business. Senior, on the other hand, was eager to sell at those prices and grew increasingly frustrated with each declined offer. The two co-owners could not agree on the sale amount and eventually had a serious falling-out.

This issue can be more challenging in situations where the co-owners have dissimilar ownership percentages. If the co-owners have equal (or close to equal) ownership percentages, the only question is, will the equal amount everybody stands to receive be sufficient for each co-owner? If the co-owners have significantly unequal ownership percentages, the co-owners with smaller portions will receive proportionately less at exit, typically making it harder for them to reach their financial goals.

Example: Plain Vanilla Inc. had two co-owners: Majority, who founded the business and owned 90 percent, and Minority, who received his 10 percent stake upon joining the company about a year after it started. Twenty years later, the two co-owners had built a highly successful business together and contemplated selling to an outside buyer. Majority felt deeply troubled that although his expected share of the sale proceeds would be more than sufficient to fund his financial goals, his long-time partner Minority's 10 percent share would leave him likely needing a new job. In response, Majority contemplated granting Minority an additional 10 percent or 20 percent stake in the business prior to sale. However, the additional ownership would not be sufficient to eliminate Minority from the need to continue working and would trigger a significant amount of taxes.

4. Legacy

The fourth major goal is Legacy. Legacy can be difficult to define and apply, and is rarely as simple as wanting the business to survive after an owner's exit. Most owners have nuanced feelings beyond the business's simple continuance. As an insightful exercise, ask yourself if you can think of a competitor to whom you would never sell your business. Many owners can.

The competitor that comes to mind does so because you believe its values or leaders would undermine what you have built within your company. That is legacy.

It can be helpful to understand Legacy as having two parts: first, *in what condition* do you wish to leave your business? Second, *to whom* do you want to leave your business? Listed below are examples of common legacy goals that reveal either a certain business condition achieved at exit or a certain business leadership situation at exit:

- ❖ "I want to leave my business strongly positioned for continued growth."
- ❖ "I want my business culture to continue after my exit."
- ❖ "I want our company's reputation and brand to favorably continue in the marketplace."
- ❖ "I want to financially reward my top employees upon my exit."
- ❖ "I want the business to be in good hands after my exit."
- ❖ "I want employees to be treated with dignity and respect."
- ❖ "I want to make sure customer needs are met after my exit."
- ❖ "I want the organization to be financially strong at the time of my exit."

Few owners would be opposed to any of the above aspirations. Where co-owners may have different and potentially incompatible views is in how they define legacy and the priority they place on achieving their legacy goals at the expense of other exit goals. For example, one co-owner might want to share ownership with key employees to reward them for their contribution to the company, whereas another co-owner may be financially unwilling or unable to do so. Or, in another example, one co-owner may want to sell to a certain buyer because that buyer offered the highest purchase price, but another co-owner may perceive that that same potential buyer would be a poor culture fit and therefore object to selling the business to that particular buyer, even at that higher price.

To achieve alignment around Legacy goals, co-owners need to discuss and define their goals as soon as possible. The more time they have prior to exit, the more options and flexibility they have to bring their goals into alignment and thus create successful exits.

5. Transition

The fifth and final major goal is Transition. This means how *involved* an owner wants to be during and after exit, including how *control* is to be handled. Many owners have strong feelings about how their role should transition during and after exit. Some owners prefer to quickly depart the business after exit, either to pursue other interests and/or to make a clear delineation between them and the new business owners. Other owners prefer to remain involved with the company after exit, usually in a limited capacity such as a chairperson, consultant, or to focus on working with a handpicked set of customers. Also, owners may have strong feelings about how control is to be addressed during transition, especially in situations where the business is being passed to a family member or sold to an inside buyer.

> *Example:* Co-Owner One desired to sell his 75 percent interest in his insurance agency to Co-Owners Two and Three, who together held the remaining 25 percent interest. Two and Three were eager to have operating control of the business, for they possessed ambitious growth plans and privately believed that One had fallen out of touch with the business's employees and customers. Co-Owner One was unwilling to give up operational control until his interest had been bought down to 25 percent or less, and he wanted to continue working with several important customer accounts after the sale. Two and Three were unwilling to wait to gain operational control and did not feel comfortable allowing One to continue working with customers. Eventually, Two and Three left the business to start a competing agency, and an extended legal conflict ensued.

To review, the Five Major Exit Goals are those goals most commonly held by business owners planning for exit and with the highest potential to create incompatibilities among co-owners. Business co-owners who create alignment around these goals will go a long way in defining a clear path to successful exits for everybody involved.

VII

What Are the Seven Steps to Creating Co-Owner Alignment?

Now that we know what exit goals co-owners most commonly need to be aligned around, we can define the steps to create and sustain alignment. The Seven Steps to Creating Co-Owner Alignment are listed and explained below.

Step 1. Understand the Issues

The first step is to understand the issues: the importance of co-owners achieving successful exits, the causes of exit-goal incompatibility, and the main goals to gain alignment around. These are the topics this Guide has addressed up to this point. Understanding the issues is a critical first step because without an adequate understanding, co-owners might apply ineffective or counterproductive remedies. Exit-goal incompatibility often emerges gradually over time without the co-owners even aware that this issue has entered the relationship and is causing tension and friction. As a result, co-owners (and their advisors and close family members) often misdiagnose the situation, usually concluding that some other issue is the culprit. As long as the true issue goes undiagnosed, the co-owners will at best treat the symptoms but not the root cause. To apply the correct solution, we must understand the true nature of the issues. As twentieth century inventor Charles Kettering said, "A problem well stated is a problem half-solved." A thorough review of this Guide and the Fable preceding it should provide co-owners with a sound basis for understanding.

Step 2. Establish Which Co-Owners Will Be Involved and to What Degree

To create exit-goal alignment among business co-owners, the second step is to determine which co-owners are involved in the planning and decision-making process, and to what degree. In some situations, this is fairly obvious—such as with two co-owners who each hold an equal fifty-fifty stake. Barring an agreement to the contrary, fifty-fifty co-owners commonly have equal involvement and decision-making authority when pursuing their exit plan. Other situations, however, may be less clear.

While all co-owners have certain rights and expectations that come with ownership, when it comes to creating orderly and successful exits, not all co-owners are created equal. The most obvious example is when one co-owner has a majority, controlling interest in the business. That majority co-owner's exit goals usually will take priority over other co-owners' goals. However, to determine which co-owners will be involved in the exit-planning process and to what degree, it is not as simple as looking at who owns what percent of the company. There are a variety of scenarios where a co-owner may be given preferential involvement or decision-making authority at this point in time, regardless of the size of his ownership interest. Examples of this include:

❖ A founding co-owner's exit goals are given preferential status out of respect for his contribution, reputation, and legacy.

❖ A co-owner who is the parent of some or all of the other co-owners may be given preferential status out of familial respect and relations.

❖ A co-owner who is seriously ill or injured may be given preferential status, and his exit goals are given first and highest priority out of altruism.

❖ Certain co-owners may possess legal rights and obligations owed to them by way of the nature of their ownership, such as participants of employee stock-ownership plans (ESOPs), co-owners holding preferred stock within corporations, or co-owners holding voting interests whereas other co-owners hold nonvoting interests.

To create exit-goal alignment, ideally the co-owners will reach consensus on whose exit goals will be assigned the higher priority at this time and whose will be of secondary or tertiary importance.

Example: *So and So Company Inc. had three co-owners: Father who owned 60 percent, Daughter who owned 15 percent, and the late founder's elderly widow who still owned 25 percent. Father wished to pass the business to Daughter. Typically, this involves implementing tactics to establish the lowest defensible company value in order to reduce potential transfer taxes upon passing the company to Daughter. However, these tactics could undermine Widow's opportunity to receive a full and fair price for her business share anytime soon. In deference to her, Father and Daughter agreed that buying out Widow's share at full and fair price was the highest priority at this time, and their exit goals would be addressed at a later date (even though combined they held 75 percent of the company).*

To help create clarity, we recommend grouping the co-owners into the following three tiers to define expectations and parameters around roles and input in the exit-planning process. The three tiers are:

Tier 1 Determinants – Co-owners whose individual exit goals will *determine* to the fullest extent possible the exit tactics to be pursued at this time, as long as pursuing their goals does not harm the rights and interests of the remaining co-owners.

Tier 2 Considerants – Co-owners whose individual exit goals will be *taken into consideration* when determining the exit tactics to be pursued at this time. Reasonable efforts may be made to pursue their exit goals at this time, as long as those efforts do not hinder or block achieving the exit goals of the Tier 1 Determinant(s).

Tier 3 Beneficiaries – Co-owners in this group are expected to proportionately *benefit* from any exit tactics pursued. However, their individual exit goals are not specifically taken into consideration at this time.

Example: *Do-Something Corporation had approximately thirty co-owners, consisting of a majority co-owner who was CEO and held 65 percent, a CFO who held 10 percent, and about twenty-eight additional co-owners who collectively held the remaining 25 percent. These additional co-owners were a mix of friends and family who invested in the business. CEO determined it was time to sell the business in anticipation of his retirement. (Thus, CEO was a Tier 1 Determinant.) CFO was a highly valued employee, but because she was significantly younger than the CEO, she was not ready to retire. Therefore, she preferred to sell the business to a buyer who offered her an attractive post-sale career path. Out of loyalty to her, CEO took her goals into consideration, such that potential buyers were specifically* *questioned about how they would employ CFO after a sale. (Thus, CFO was a Tier 2 Considerant.) The remaining co-owners were not individually involved in the exit-planning and sale process, but they would proportionately benefit from a successful sale of the company. (Thus, these co-owners were Tier 3 Beneficiaries.)*

Sometimes determining which co-owners belong in which tiers is a straightforward matter readily agreed upon by all the co-owners. Yet in other situations, co-owners may have conflicting opinions. The three tiers should be taken as guidelines that are useful to create clarity and set co-owner expectations, not as hard and fast delineations. In these situations, it may be advantageous to use a professional facilitator to help the co-owners reach consensus on these issues.

Step 3. Co-Owners Determine Their Preliminary Individual Exit Goals and Priorities

The third step to create co-owner alignment is for each co-owner directly involved in the process (Tier 1 and Tier 2 co-owners) to draft a preliminary list of his or her individual exit goals in order of priority. It is impossible to know if the co-owners collectively have compatible or incompatible goals until the individual owners achieve a preliminary understanding of what their goals may be in a ranking of importance. At this step, co-owners should consider their individual exit goals to only be preliminary statements, because the goals might be modified once all of the involved co-owners come together to share and compare their goals (see Step 4 below).

Some co-owners enjoy such a high degree of trust and transparency that they may be comfortable working on their goals as a group exercise right from the start. However, most co-owners benefit from some period of individual research and reflection. Also, it is important for individual owners to receive input from their close family members and advisors during this process. For these reasons, it is important that individual co-owners spend sufficient time apart from their peers to discern their tentative exit goals and priorities.

The Five Major Goals reviewed in the previous section of this Guide are usually the most important to define, because they are the most commonly held exit goals and usually have the highest potential for causing incompatibility. However, every business owner is different, and therefore every owner will have a unique set of exit goals. Some owners can readily determine and articulate their exit goals, while others need time and assistance. Ideally, owners should start this process long before their desired exit in order to give themselves sufficient time for research, personal reflection, and input from loved ones and advisors.

Example: J. R. was the majority co-owner of a successful software company. While he knew he wanted to exit sometime within the next five to ten years, he was unable to clearly define a set of exit goals and priorities. Over several months, J. R. sought out several other business owners who had already exited and asked them about their experiences. He also read several books about the subject and consulted with his advisors. Finally, he and his spouse attended a weekend retreat specifically conducted to prepare business owners for exit. By the end of this process, J. R. believed he established a preliminary set of clear exit goals for himself, his family, and his business.

Step 4. Co-Owners Share Goals and Address Incompatibilities

Once co-owners have formulated their tentative, individual exit goals, the next step is to share and compare their goals and priorities with one another. This can be the most difficult step. Sharing exit goals presents significant risks:

- ❖ Sharing may require co-owners to reveal personal and private information, aspirations, fears, and feelings.
- ❖ Incompatibilities may be exposed that, up to that point, were either unknown or have been "the elephant in the room."
- ❖ Sharing goals can feel selfish, for it necessitates that co-owners assert what they want, perhaps after many years of putting the business or the team first.
- ❖ Once shared, one co-owner's exit goals may disappoint or upset other co-owners, even if the goals are not necessarily incompatible.

Example: Two equal co-owners, Red and Black, built a successful trucking business, working side by side for twenty-five years. Along the way, they bought and profitably sold several pieces of commercial real estate. Red was eager to sell the trucking business, and with his sale proceeds he intended to launch his own commercial real estate investment company. Black was also eager to sell their trucking business, but he expected they would continue forward as partners again in any new ventures. Black was surprised and hurt to learn that Red did not wish to be his partner again after the sale.

There are a variety of methods one can use to implement this step. Some co-owners' initial instinct is to file into a room and just take turns laying on the table their draft goals and priorities. However, this approach is risky even among the most collegial co-owners, and once started cannot be undone. Therefore, it is highly advisable to use a third party, typically a professional exit planner, to lead the co-owners through this step. An exit planner can serve as a go-between for the co-owners, provide an objective voice, reduce tension, ensure that every involved co-owner has a chance to contribute, and immediately identify tactics that enhance alignment. We recommend the following four-part approach to compare co-owner exit goals and address incompatibilities:

1. The exit planner confidentially interviews the individual co-owners (Tier 1 and 2) and, if necessary, assists with the formation of individual preliminary exit goals and priorities.

2. The planner collects the co-owners' tentative exit goals and reviews them privately. This allows the exit planner to identify in advance potential areas of incompatibility and areas where the co-owners already are in alignment.

3. The exit planner then meets again with the co-owners individually and privately. Acting as an objective and confidential mediator, the exit planner can suggest opportunities to build alignment by offering points of compromise and recommending tactics that create alignment. The exit planner may repeat this effort several times to narrow gaps and build agreement.

4. Finally, the exit planner brings the co-owners together as a group only when the individual co-owners feel prepared and when the planner has identified solutions to address any remaining incompatible goals.

In nearly all situations, getting to alignment requires negotiation and compromise. Sometimes this involves nothing more than adjusting goals and rearranging priorities to reduce and eliminate the potential for any single co-owner's exit goals to go unrealized or interfere with another's goals. To facilitate this, the co-owners' outside advisors will bring their experience and objectivity to the negotiation and reconciliation process.

Example: Co-Owner Up wanted to sell his 70 percent ownership stake to Co-Owner Down, who held the remaining 30 percent of the business. Initially, Up drafted a set of exit goals that included selling his share of the business for "not one penny below $10 million" in an all-cash transaction and receiving a five-year guaranteed employment contract with the company post-sale. The exit planner met privately with Down and introduced Up's preliminary goals. Down believed the price and terms were *so unreasonable that he threatened to immediately quit. The exit planner convinced Down to remain with the company and work toward an aligned outcome. After several rounds of discussions, Up remained committed to his $10 million asking price, but he dropped his demand for an all-cash deal and expressed willingness to be paid over five years. Up also agreed to drop his demand for a guaranteed employment contract, and instead was willing to accept a performance-based, annually renewable consulting agreement. Down still believed the $10 million price was excessive. However, Down finally agreed to purchase Up's interest at that price because the other concessions reduced Down's risk in the transaction.*

In other situations, the path to alignment is not easily discernable and may require more than simply negotiating concessions to adjust goals and priorities. At that point, advisors experienced in working with privately owned businesses and their co-owners may need to suggest business, legal, accounting, financial, and compensation-related tools and tactics that help bridge gaps and create mutually beneficial outcomes.

Example: Co-Owner White wanted over the next five to ten years to sell his 80 percent interest to Co-Owner Blue, who held the remaining 20 percent and was a key employee within the business. Blue wanted to purchase the company, but Blue had serious concerns about the price he would have to pay when the time came. The business was rapidly growing in size, in large part due to Blue's leadership. Blue worried that his efforts were only inflating the future price he would have to pay for White's stake. In response, their exit advisors helped the two co-owners implement a buyout agreement which applied a discount to Blue's future purchase price in proportion to the company growth that Blue created. The more Blue increased company growth between now and White's exit, the greater the discount Blue received on the eventual purchase price. Thus, both co-owners stood to gain as the business increased in size and value.

Step 5. Address and Eliminate Alignment Inhibitors

Once business co-owners have started their exit planning, they may discover that there are certain practices occurring (or not occurring) within their company that make alignment more difficult. These practices, called Alignment Inhibitors, usually seem harmless or sometimes even beneficial, but as exit draws near, they unknowingly and unintentionally inhibit co-owner exit alignment. The more Alignment Inhibitors found within a company, the more difficult it is to create and maintain co-owner exit alignment. Therefore, while drafting and sharing co-owner exit goals and priorities, it is helpful and important to eliminate Alignment Inhibitors where possible.

There are six Alignment Inhibitors commonly encountered within small to medium privately held companies. Each Inhibitor and its potential impact is described below.

1. Co-Owners Working in the Business without Written Job Descriptions

Co-owners working in the business often exempt themselves from this common employee management tool under the premise that the document is unnecessary because they are owners first and employees second. However, it is difficult for co-owners to achieve and maintain alignment if their roles and responsibilities within the company are unwritten and thus left up to individual interpretation and application.

When co-owners do not have current written job descriptions, a common byproduct is a blurring decision-making authority and accountability. This, in turn, reduces efficiency and increases co-owner tension. It is easy to envision the problems created if every company decision and issue were subject to a vote of the co-owners. Not all co-owners can be—nor should be—involved in all decisions. Some issues are ownership-level matters that require discussion and input from the co-owners. Other issues are management-level matters dealing with day-to-day operational and tactical areas. Yet without written job descriptions, which co-owner has input and authority to make which decisions and in which circumstances remains unspecified. This ambiguity invites co-owners to interpret the answers for themselves—not a method that leads to alignment.

Co-owners can rely on precedent and ad hoc efforts to fumble their way through this ambiguity for a surprisingly long time, as long as their goals are in alignment. But, when exit draws near for one or more co-owners and their goals change, co-owners are left open to reinterpret their responsibilities and reevaluate their priorities as they see fit. At that point, the lack of written job descriptions can cause significant co-owner difficulties and inhibit creating exit-goal alignment.

Example: Acme Company had two co-owners: Apple (75 percent) and Orange (25 percent). Orange intended to buy out Apple at a future point in time. One day, one of Orange's top salespersons came to him with the news that this salesperson had received a job offer from a competitor. The salesperson did not want to leave, but Orange would have to raise this salesperson's compensation by $50,000 to match the competitor's offer. Orange believed the loss of this salesperson's production would seriously *hinder his ability to buy Apple's interest. Up to that point, Orange freely made hiring and compensation decisions for the sales team. Orange intended to match the competitor's offer, but Apple vetoed the decision. Apple objected to the compensation amount, saying authority to approve the raise was his, given its size and immediately detrimental impact on company profitability. Apple believed that the sale of his interest would not be adversely impacted in the long term. The two co-owners found themselves in a contentious dispute, and Orange eventually withdrew from purchasing Apple's interest.*

2. Co-Owners Working in the Business without Job Performance Benchmarks and Evaluations

As with the previous inhibitor, co-owners working in the business often exempt themselves from written job performance benchmarks and periodic evaluations against those benchmarks under the premise that the exercises are unnecessary given that they are business owners. In situations where the co-owners are equal partners, a further reason this inhibitor occurs is the equal co-owners may find it difficult to evaluate one another's job performance and hold one another accountable for performance, given that they see themselves more as peers and not subordinate to one another. When this inhibitor occurs, co-owners may struggle to gain alignment because each co-owner is left to individually interpret not only his or her responsibilities and performance, but each other's as well. This fuels misunderstanding and a lack of accountability. As exit draws near, co-owners develop different goals and shift their activities, consciously or not, to support their new desired outcomes. As a result, co-owners working in the business are now pursuing different goals, but lack the tools to recognize this and address it in a constructive manner.

Example: Main Street Company had three co-owners: Father, who held 80 percent, and Two Children who each held 10 percent ownership. All three co-owners wanted the business to pass down from Father to Two Children. Part of Father's historical responsibilities included managing relations with more than a dozen of the oldest and largest customer accounts. Recognizing the risk this presented at Father's exit, Two Children secured Father's agreement that handing off those relationships to others in the organization was the highest priority. However, Father had no specific job performance benchmarks, and therefore was left to determine for himself how to migrate these customer relationships and at what pace. As months and eventually a couple years went by, Father believed he was making good progress, for he had introduced other employees into several of the accounts. However, most of the accounts continued to directly interact with him. Two Children felt Father's pace was unnecessarily slow, but they were unwilling to insist on specific performance benchmarks out of deference to him as their parent and majority co-owner. Eventually, Two Children concluded that Father was unwilling to give up control. To Father's surprise and disappointment, Two Children left to start a new company on their own.

3. Tying Co-Owner Compensation to Ownership Share Rather Than Market Rates

This is a common Alignment Inhibitor among co-owners with identical ownership percentages (i.e., two co-owners with fifty-fifty ownership; three co-owners with 33 percent ownership each; etc.) and cofounders. It is also one of the most difficult inhibitors to confront. Equal co-owners usually aspire to treat themselves equally, and therefore they agree early in their relationship to allocate everything equally, including compensation. In the beginning, this seems positive and advantageous. While the business is small and cannot yet afford to pay market-rate wages to the co-owners, taking equal below-market compensation evenly spreads the risks and burden. Once revenues and profits increase, the co-owners usually enact identical wage increases, even though the co-owners evolve into different positions within the company. If this continues unabated, the co-owners end up with wages grossly inconsistent with market rates for the position each occupies. This puts unhealthy pressure on co-owners trying to create aligned exit plans.

Example: *Alpha and Beta were fifty-fifty co-owners and cofounders of a twenty-year-old retail business doing approximately $30 million in revenue. Alpha served as the company's chief executive since founding. His wages were $250,000 per year, even though the market rate for his position was approximately double that figure. Beta's title was vice president, but his responsibilities over the years never moved further than managing inventory buying. Beta's wages were also $250,000 per year, even though the market rate for his position was closer to $100,000. Over time, Alpha increasingly resented the imbalance. His compensation was $250,000 less per year than he could have earned elsewhere, and the $150,000 annual overpayment to Beta reduced Alpha's profit distributions by $75,000 per year. Alpha eventually sought to sell the company earlier than he otherwise preferred, for he was unable to tolerate the financial imbalance and unwilling to confront his co-owner on the matter.*

It is not difficult to see the negative pressure this exerts on the co-owner relationship, regardless of how well the co-owners work together. Even the most good-natured and selfless underpaid co-owners may feel pressure to exit in order to get out of the undesirable situation. Grossly overpaid co-owners usually fail to see any issues; in fairness, they are adhering to an arrangement that all the co-owners willingly entered into years earlier. Co-owners significantly overpaid for their position are often less inclined to exit from the business, because they are earning wages higher than they likely would earn in a different situation.

While it would be easy to conclude that the solution should be co-owners simply need to adjust compensation to be consistent with market rates for the positions they occupy, this is easier said than done. Once this genie is out of the bottle, it is difficult to get it back inside. Underpaid co-owners are understandably unwilling to take pay cuts (and are sometimes offended by the very suggestion). Overpaid co-owners often feel that they entered into an arrangement and need to stand by it. Furthermore, overpaid co-owners often resist addressing the matter for fear of harming co-owner relations. What is important to understand from an exit perspective is that paying equal compensation based on equal ownership inhibits co-owner alignment because it puts unequal pressure on those co-owners to exit.

The proper place for business co-owners with equal ownership to treat themselves equally is with profit distributions. Profits are surplus earnings to either be reinvested or distributed for the benefit of the business's owners. When distributed, profits are usually shared in proportion to ownership (unless their ownership structure or a prior agreement dictates otherwise). Wages, on the other hand, are different. Wages are payments to people for services rendered to the business. Wages should be consistent with market rates for similar positions and for persons with similar skills and experiences.

4. No Long-Term Strategic Planning Process or Written Strategic Plan

Many businesses manage to achieve significant revenue and profit increases without formal long-term strategic plans or planning processes. Therefore, to some owners, strategic planning and plans seem unnecessary, wasteful of time, and potentially counterproductive if the process creates rigidity in the company. However, as one or more co-owners approach exit, the lack of a disciplined approach to strategic planning frequently inhibits co-owner alignment. As exit draws near, different co-owners may develop different objectives for the company's growth and direction. For example, a co-owner seeking to sell his or her interest in the near future may want to pursue initiatives that have the potential to rapidly increase business results, all in order to drive up the sale price. A co-owner not seeking to exit soon may take a longer-term view and wish to pursue strategies that provide for steadier and more sustainable growth. In another example, co-owners contemplating exit may see the need to increase debt or take on outside investors to provide capital for accelerated growth, whereas co-owners not exiting soon may be opposed to capital strategies that increase risk or cause dilution. As we have seen, there is no universally right nor wrong position—only co-owners with different goals.

An effective long-term strategic planning process requires co-owners (and their leadership team) to debate and determine a unified course of action for the business. Their decisions are summarized in a written document—the strategic plan—to share within the organization to increase buy-in and enhance accountability. Without an effective planning process, co-owners often find themselves pursuing individual initiatives and ideas, pulling the organization in different directions and undermining or outright sabotaging alignment.

> **Example:** *No-Name Industries had three co-owners. One co-owner served as the CEO, while the other two co-owners each lead a business unit, the Red Unit and Blue Unit. Both business units were profitable and growing. However, the Red Unit was twice the size of the Blue Unit, while the Blue Unit was growing twice as fast. All three co-owners shunned any formal approach to strategic planning as unnecessary and overly bureaucratic, preferring instead to be "nimble and opportunistic" in the marketplace. Thus, the co-owners who lead the Red and Blue Units would individually lobby the CEO for additional resources to grow their respective units as those resources became available. Over time, the co-owner leading the Blue Unit grew increasingly frustrated. He believed his business unit, while smaller, justified greater resources given its higher growth rate. The competition between the two units eventually evolved into conflict between the co-owners. Finally, the co-owner leading the Blue Unit quit the company and launched a competing organization.*

5. No Financial Budget and/or Periodic Performance Reviews against That Budget

Businesses can achieve significant revenue and profit increases without preparing an annual budget or without periodically evaluating performance against a budget they may create. Therefore, to some owners budgeting seems to be a waste of time and unnecessary. However, a well-thought-out and actively reviewed budget is an important tool to create co-owner alignment. Just as with a strategic planning process, the budgeting process requires co-owners to debate and determine how they will annually allocate financial resources and in what priorities. The finished product—the written budget—serves as the financial song sheet for the co-owners (and their leadership team) to sing from. In organizations lacking a healthy budgeting process, co-owners likely find themselves engaged in an ongoing tug-of-war over the next surplus dollar and discretionary expense.

> **Example:** *Everyday Business Inc. had four equal co-owners and cofounders. Each of the four had a distinct and different job within the organization. It happened that the eldest co-owner served as the CFO, while the CEO was the youngest co-owner—she was more than ten years younger than the CFO. Ever since starting the company, CFO made periodic cash distributions in equal amounts to the four co-owners entirely at his discretion. In the beginning, the company was small and thus the distributions were modest and infrequent. Over time, the distributions grew more regular, ultimately settling into routine quarterly distributions. As time went by, CEO sought to accelerate business growth with an eye toward a future sale. To fund the accelerated growth, she wanted to reduce or eliminate the distributions and increase reinvestment back into the business. This required her to lobby her co-owners each quarter to reduce or skip the regular distribution. The CEO co-owner found the process inefficient and stressful. Worse, her three other co-owners adopted a position that the decision to fund her growth initiatives had to be unanimous, or they would default to the full distribution for that quarter. CEO concluded she could not grow the company in that environment. After an unsuccessful attempt to buy out the other co-owners, she left the organization.*

6. No Regular Co-Owner-Only Meetings

Co-owners of small- to medium-sized businesses are notoriously inconsistent about conducting regular meetings for just the company's co-owners. Many co-owners are comfortable dispensing with the formalities of regularly held meetings, especially if all of the co-owners are actively involved in the business. When co-owners work inside the company, they may see little need for dedicated meetings for the co-owners separate and apart from the business's leadership team, because they likely know most of what is happening within the company and are busy dealing with pressing issues and priorities.

Making matters worse, since the 1990s and 2000s, the limited liability company (LLC) has become the most prevalent legal form for businesses within the United States. Before then, the most common legal business form was corporations: regular C and subchapter S corporations. Corporations must have clearly designated boards of directors and officers and must hold regular owner (i.e., "shareholder") meetings at least once per year. In contrast, LLCs usually are not legally required to name boards of directors and officers, nor are they required to hold meetings among owners (i.e., "members"). Thus, business co-owners today have even lower sensitivity to the need to hold regular co-owner meetings than was true in the past.

To understand how the absence of a regular schedule of co-owner-only meetings inhibits co-owner alignment, we must return to the distinction between *ownership-level* decisions and *management-level* decisions. "Should we sell the company?" is an ownership-level decision in most owners' eyes. "Do we upgrade our photocopy machines?" is probably a management-level decision. Without a set schedule of co-owner-only meetings, the co-owners lack a regular forum to discuss, debate, and decide ownership-level issues. Without this forum, alignment is undermined in several ways. First, too often those ownership-level decisions are pushed into the future in lieu of dealing with more urgent (but perhaps less important) matters. Second, it is difficult to maintain trust and good relations among co-owners if they lack regular opportunities for ownership-level conversations. As Susan Scott wrote in her book *Fierce Conversations*, "The conversations are the relationship." Without regular conversations, the co-owner relationships suffer.

> **Example:** *XYZ Enterprises, LLC had a total of six co-owners consisting of Primary co-owner, who held 60 percent of the company, and five Key Employees, who collectively held the remaining 40 percent. All of the co-owners worked closely together within the business, but they had not met for ownership-level discussions in years. As Primary began to work on his exit goals, he realized that, as part of his legacy, he wanted to expand ownership to an additional group of employees in order to motivate and retain the next generation of the company's top young talent. However, Primary did not want to dilute his ownership below 60 percent.*
>
> *Therefore, Primary convened for the first time in many years a meeting of all the current co-owners. At this meeting, he surprised the five Key Employees and extended a written offer to buy ownership from them so that he could offer ownership to a new group of employees without diluting himself. Two of the Key Employees immediately expressed suspicion. They asked why the unprecedented offer was being made at that time. Was there something on*

the horizon that would cause the company to rapidly increase in value, and Primary sought to buy them out before this event occurred? Why was Primary so unwilling to dilute himself? Who would determine which other employees would be offered ownership? The questions asked by the two Key Employees unnerved the remaining minority co-owners, and as a result, none agreed to sell a portion of their interest. Primary thus was not only unable to create an ownership opportunity for a new group of employees, but he also found himself having to address a disgruntled and suspicious group of minority co-owners.

There are other ways business co-owners may be operating their businesses and relating to each other which inhibit alignment. However, the six Alignment Inhibitors discussed here are the most common and can present the biggest challenges to overcome. It is important to emphasize that Alignment Inhibitors seem to cause little harm or even be advantageous in the present, while the co-owners are working side by side with a common goal of growing the business. However, once one or more co-owners nears exit, these Alignment Inhibitors can hinder or outright block the co-owners' ability to create exit alignment.

Step 6. Implement Alignment Creators

Just as co-owners may do (and not do) certain things to inhibit alignment among themselves, there are certain things co-owners can do to foster alignment. Alignment Creators are practices, habits, and processes which help co-owners initially create and subsequently sustain alignment—both now and up to exit.

Many Alignment Creators are tools commonly used to run a well-managed company. Thus, many businesses have in place some of these mechanisms for reasons unrelated to preparing for exit. However, co-owners may gain a new and deeper appreciation once they understand the important role these tools play in achieving co-owner alignment and exit success. Other Alignment Creators are less familiar and more specialized.

The next seven pages lists two dozen Alignment Creators and offers a brief explanation of how each is used and its potential benefits.

Table 2:

Alignment Creators and a Brief Explanation of How Each Is Used and Its Potential Benefits

Description	How It Helps Create Co-Owner Alignment
Owner-Only Meetings Regularly scheduled meetings (not less than annual) reserved for business co-owners. The suggested agenda includes reviewing business performance and leadership and discussing and deciding upon ownership-related issues.	Provides co-owners with a forum to proactively, regularly, and openly evaluate business performance and address issues that impact them and their interest in the company.
Perks and Benefits Policy Written guidelines governing perks and benefits that co-owners may receive from the company, such as vehicles, travel, meals, expense allowances, etc. Usually will list appropriate categories, set financial limits, and stipulate accounting practices.	Avoids unregulated or imbalanced co-owner discretionary spending, which can lead to co-owner friction and conflict.
Responsibilities Policy Written guidelines stipulating the responsibilities co-owners agree to uphold to protect and support the business. Potentially includes guidelines or policies covering conflict-of-interest, personal guarantees of business debt, loans to co-owners, nepotism, and capital calls.	Sets clear and balanced expectations among co-owners regarding the responsibilities that come with ownership. Protects the business from decisions or actions by any one co-owner that could harm the business and/or the other co-owners.
Reinvest-Receive Guidelines Written guidelines, typically updated once per year, to define what portion of available surplus cash will be reinvested back into the business and what portion the co-owners will receive from the business.	Sets clear expectations among co-owners, avoids ad hoc or reactionary decision-making, and ensures the business has sufficient capital for sustained growth.

Table 2 Continued:
Alignment Creators and a Brief Explanation
of How Each Is Used and Its Potential Benefits

Description	How It Helps Create Co-Owner Alignment
Ownership Expansion Guidelines Written guidelines defining the criteria and circumstances under which the existing co-owners would consider welcoming additional co-owners into the business. Usually stipulates eligibility, background and qualifications, and buy-in terms.	Sets clear expectations among existing co-owners and owner aspirants, defines the decision-making process and authority, and protects existing co-owner rights.
Purchase-Sale Window Regularly scheduled periods where existing co-owners seeking to increase or decrease their ownership may approach the business and/or one another to conduct a transaction. Often open once per year for a defined period (such as thirty days).	Commonly used in companies with a larger number of co-owners to provide a semi-regular market for the co-owners' interests. Sets a defined period and process to facilitate buy-ups or buy-downs between interested co-owners or the business itself.
Ownership Options Options given to individuals working in the business who seek to become co-owners or increase their current ownership interest. Usually requires a minimum length of service, job performance, and/or company growth.	Gives incent to both employees to become co-owners and existing co-owners working in the business to drive company growth. Also provides a clear path for persons to increase ownership should they desire.
Buy-Sell Agreement Legal document governing ownership changes between co-owners, such as in the event of a co-owner death, serious disability, or separation from employment. Typically includes provisions for establishing price, terms, and funding for any transactions. Should be reviewed at least annually and updated as necessary.	Prevents ownership from being sold or transferred to unwanted individuals, creates a clear path for co-owners interested in increasing ownership in the future, and provides a process for buying out co-owners who are deceased or no longer willing or able to remain involved with the business.

Table 2 Continued:
Alignment Creators and a Brief Explanation
of How Each Is Used and Its Potential Benefits

Description	How It Helps Create Co-Owner Alignment
Co-Owner Retreats Extended offsite meetings, often up to several days in length, conducted by a facilitator experienced in exit issues. May include spouses.	Dedicated private time allowing co-owners to focus on important issues and decisions impacting business growth, business value, and exit success.
Drag-Along and Tag-Along Rights Provisions within a buy-sell agreement that bind co-owners together to act in concert upon sale of the business. Drag-along rights ensure that a controlling co-owner can deliver to a buyer a business free of minority holdouts. Tag-along rights ensure that a minority co-owner will not be left behind by a controlling co-owner.	Protects the co-owners' rights and investment value within the business.
Employee Agreements A formal agreement that specifies the conditions of the relationship between an employee and an employer. Unlike employment contracts, which typically are executed for a specified period of time and may be guaranteed, employee agreements usually provide no guaranteed employment period nor compensation levels. Includes noncompete, nonsolicitation, and nondisclosure provisions where possible. Advantageous to use with all persons employed within the business, including co-owners working within the business.	Sets clear expectations about the requirements and conditions for employment within the business and protects the company from any hostile actions of former employees.

Table 2 Continued:
Alignment Creators and a Brief Explanation
of How Each Is Used and Its Potential Benefits

Description	How It Helps Create Co-Owner Alignment
Operating Agreements (LLCs only) A formal agreement among co-owners of limited liability companies (LLCs), called members, to govern the LLC's conduct. Most US states require LLCs to have an operating agreement. Topics addressed often include decision-making authority and process, rights and duties, distribution of profits, and tax responsibilities.	Defines each co-owner's rights, powers, and benefits. Clearly sets and communicates the management authority within the LLC.
Partnership Agreements (partnerships only) A formal agreement among co-owners in a partnership, called partners, to govern the partnership's conduct. The agreement stipulates the partners' obligations and contributions to the partnership. Topics addressed often include decision-making authority and process, rights and duties, distributions of profits, and tax responsibilities.	Defines each co-owner's rights, powers, and benefits. Clearly sets and communicates the management authority within the partnership.
Corporate Bylaws (corporations only) A formal agreement among co-owners in a corporation, called shareholders, to govern the corporation's conduct. Bylaws stipulate the rights and powers of the shareholders, directors, and officers. Topics addressed often include the meeting schedule for shareholders, officer title and compensation, and decision-making authority within the corporation.	Defines each co-owner's rights, powers, and benefits. Clearly sets and communicates the management authority within the corporation.
Values Statements A written statement of the business's core beliefs, top priorities, and/or aspirational norms and behaviors. Often used to help the business connect with customers, employees, and the community.	Helps co-owners define and adhere to a shared set of principles and norms to be applied in conduct with employees, customers, and each other.

Table 2 Continued:
Alignment Creators and a Brief Explanation
of How Each Is Used and Its Potential Benefits

Description	How It Helps Create Co-Owner Alignment
Job Descriptions Written summary of the purpose, responsibilities, authority level, and reporting relationships for a certain position within a business. Advantageous to use with all persons employed within the business, including co-owners working within the business.	Sets clear expectations about the requirements and conditions for holding that position within the business and the responsibilities associated with that position.
Performance Benchmarks and Reviews Regular evaluation of an employee's conduct and quality of work as compared to a set of previously determined, measurable goals and standards. Goals and standards may be individual, collective, or both. Reviews are typically conducted not less than annually and include clear consequences for performance above and below the benchmarks. Advantageous to use with all persons employed within the business, including co-owners working within the business.	Sets clear expectations for the desired quality of work from the person occupying that position within the business and the consequences if the results are above or below expectations.
Compensation Guidelines Written description of the wages and benefits associated with a given position within the business. Often expressed as range of values, and the actual compensation applied will fall within that range based on job performance and employee experience and skills. Should be periodically evaluated against market rates for comparable positions within similar organizations.	Sets clear expectations about the requirements and conditions for holding that position within the business and the compensation that may be earned from that position.

Table 2 Continued:
Alignment Creators and a Brief Explanation of How Each Is Used and Its Potential Benefits

Description	How It Helps Create Co-Owner Alignment
Vision and Mission Statement Written statements that articulate the business's beliefs, values, and reason for existence. They establish the business's long-term direction and goals. The two statements may also express aspirational outcomes, define target audiences and customers, and provide an overview of the products and services offered.	Helps co-owners define and adhere to a commonly shared understanding of business purpose and direction.
Organizational Chart Written overview, often graphical, of the key positions and functions within a business, department, or unit, and their relationship to one another. Used to determine and maintain the most efficient leadership and staffing structure for the organization.	Helps co-owners determine and evaluate leadership roles and responsibilities and chain of command within the business.
Business Growth Plan (a.k.a. Strategic Plan) A written document that pairs the business's major long-term (commonly three to five years) objectives with the needs of its marketplace, then describes the strategies and tactics that will lead to achieving those objectives. Often includes analysis of market needs, industry trends, and competitor positions. Ideally performance against the plan is periodically measured, not less than annually.	Helps co-owners determine and communicate the business's strategic direction and priorities, and keeps the company's leaders on track and accountable to meet those objectives. Also helps co-owners determine capital needed to achieve the objectives.

Table 2 Continued:
Alignment Creators and a Brief Explanation
of How Each Is Used and Its Potential Benefits

Description	How It Helps Create Co-Owner Alignment
Annual Budget Written statement of the business's anticipated future financial performance, typically within the immediate calendar or fiscal year. Usually itemizes and sets objectives for all important revenue and expense categories. Ideally performance against the budget is periodically measured, usually quarterly or monthly.	Helps co-owners determine and communicate the business's short-term (up to one year) financial performance goals and expectations and keeps the company's leaders on track and accountable to meet those goals. Also helps co-owners determine capital needed to sustain the desired growth rate.
Dashboards/Scoreboards Reports designed to provide at a glance frequent business performance and results in a small number of key areas. Typically updated weekly or daily. Ideally focuses on activities which are leading indicators of success.	Helps co-owners frequently monitor key performance areas and keep the company's leaders on track and accountable to meet desired performance standards.
Board of Directors While required for corporations, many small to midsized businesses do not have boards which include independent directors selected from outside the company for their diverse expertise and perspective. Board directors are elected by the business owner(s) and typically meet six to twelve times per year. The primary roles include selecting, evaluating, and determining compensation for the chief executive officer, assessing the overall strategy and direction of the business, overseeing audits, and deciding major strategic issues such as raising debt and selling the business.	Assists co-owners in making sound, objective decisions to maximize business growth. Provides a layer of objectivity and independence separate from the co-owners and management team. Determines governance policy and structure.

Note that many of the Alignment Creators described in Table 2 may exist as stand-alone tools and documents, or may be combined. For example, a buy-sell agreement may contain drag-along and tag-along provisions.

Co-owners, with help from their advisors, are encouraged to review the list of Alignment Creators and implement those which may help produce and sustain operating and exit alignment among the co-owners.

Step 7. Monitor and Adjust with Time

Prudent business co-owners start their exit-planning years before a desired exit. During those years, one can expect that circumstances will change. Individual co-owners may experience changes to their health, marital status, family income, or other factors which could potentially cause them to reevaluate their exit goals. Additionally, the following factors may impact some or all of the co-owners: market conditions, economic environment, business performance, customer preferences, and the competitive situation.

As one or more co-owners move closer to exit, co-owners must frequently monitor exit progress, be on the alert for relevant changes, and adjust their exit tactics appropriately. Suggested methods include:

- ❖ Meet with advisors periodically to monitor existing exit plans and tactics and to address additional needs and areas for improvement.
- ❖ Maintain a written list of pending projects and tasks associated with preparing co-owners for exit, and hold advisors, employees, and co-owners responsible for results.
- ❖ Conduct an annual co-owner retreat to discuss ownership-level issues, update goals and objectives, and implement or update Alignment Creators.

VIII

Supplemental Questions

1. When should co-owners start their exit planning?

Right away. Stephen Covey noted that one of the seven habits of highly successful people is to "begin with the end in mind." So too should co-owners. There are two primary reasons to start working now on exit plans. First, there is no way to know if the decisions you make today will lead to exit success or shortfall if you do not have clearly defined exit goals. As illustrated in the Fable, many business decisions made in the present time seem to be sound and proper, but when exit draws near those decisions hinder or undermine successful exits. Second, many of the legal, tax, financial, and other tactics and tools to help co-owners exit successfully take years to implement or reach full effectiveness. The less lead time co-owners allot themselves to prepare for exit, the harder things become because they have fewer options and less flexibility. If you or your co-owners have five years or less remaining until a desired exit, it is crunch time.

2. Why should co-owners get exit-planning assistance from outside advisors?

Planning for and achieving a successful exit involves a range of financial, tax, legal, and business challenges. Also, most business owners will exit only once and consequently lack experience planning for exit. Therefore, owners and co-owners stand to greatly benefit from engaging a team of advisors knowledgeable and accomplished in this field. The essential advisors are an exit planner, accountant, and attorney. Depending on the co-owners' exit strategy and time horizon, additional advisors may include a mergers and acquisitions (M&A) professional, commercial banker, financial planner, and business appraiser.

3. What if the co-owners are related to each other?

The core message of this book is business co-owners must collaborate to achieve successful exits because their goals often will be different and incompatible; pursuing goals without alignment denies exit success to everybody. If two or more co-owners are related, this core message still applies. However, achieving alignment may be more difficult for co-owners who are related because they have to address familial history, sensitivities, and expectations on top of all the issues nonrelated business co-owners must face. The tactics and tools described in this book are available to related co-owners, and in some circumstances may be even more essential to implement.

4. What if one or more of the co-owners do not actively work in the business?

Co-owners not actively at work in the business may have a different perspective and set of exit goals, yet the core message of co-owners working together to achieve exit success still applies, particularly if they are considered Tier 1 Determinants or Tier 2 Considerants. Often, many of the Alignment Creators are even more important and impactful for co-owners not actively at work in the business because they typically are less informed about current events within the business. An important part of creating goal alignment with outside co-owners is using Alignment Creators to constructively inform and involve them where helpful and required.

5. What if one of the co-owners is an institution?

Institutional co-owners (such as private equity, family offices, or investment funds) usually have exit-goal clarity—they know with a high degree of certainty what they want to achieve from their ownership position in the business. To protect their investment and further their goals, institutional co-owners commonly mandate various legal, financial, and managerial controls that will influence or outright predetermine how the remaining individual co-owners must approach exit. This actually leaves less opportunity for misalignment between institutional and individual co-owners, simply because the institutional co-owner's goals receive highest priority. Having said that, most institutional investors will either applaud or insist upon many of the tools and tactics reviewed in this book as prudent business governance.

6. What if someone is not actually a co-owner, but is being treated as a co-owner?

There are some instances where business co-owners have an individual whom they treat as a co-owner, even though that individual does not hold actual ownership in the company. The other individual has expectations of ownership, usually because he invested in the business or is a key employee who is treated as a co-owner, but is unable or unwilling to hold actual ownership at this time due to any of several reasons:

- ❖ Professional or industry licensing requirement that cannot be met;
- ❖ Past financial or legal difficulties that preclude ownership;
- ❖ Part of an estate-tax planning strategy to reduce the size of one's taxable estate.

Regardless of the specific events leading up to the situation, the lessons and tactics outlined in this book should apply to this person alongside the other co-owners. Exit planning for this group will be more challenging and complex because these co-owners face additional tax, financial, and legal obstacles to include this person as an owner when he or she is, in fact, not an owner. Thus, business co-owners in this situation should work with experienced advisors to address these needs as early as possible.

7. What if the co-owners are struggling or resistant to talk about these issues?

To make any progress toward exit success, co-owners must have open, sincere, forthright conversations with one another and others, including family members, employees, and advisors. The conversations will cover a range of topics not commonly nor easily addressed: money, family, personal dreams and aspirations, and fears. The conversations carry the potential to do more harm than good if not conducted effectively. For these reasons, co-owners should recognize that it is normal and appropriate to have hesitations and concerns about initiating and conducting these conversations. While the co-owners' advisors can play an important role in facilitating and easing these conversations, at some point it will likely be necessary for the co-owners themselves to candidly and directly talk.

In addition to leaning on their advisors for assistance, there are other resources co-owners can utilize to prepare themselves for the required conversations. Two books this author is familiar with are *Crucial Conversations: Tools for Talking When Stakes Are High* by Kerry Patterson, and *Fierce Conversations: Achieving Success at Work and in Life One Conversation at a Time* by Susan Scott. The principles and tactics presented in these works may help co-owners prepare for and conduct more effective conversations with each other and the other persons involved in the exit process.

8. What if the co-owners are not getting along with one another?

Achieving exit success requires cooperative co-owners. A broken or contentious co-owner relationship will interfere with the communication, collaboration, and teamwork required for exit success. Ideally, co-owners who are not getting along will resolve the underlying relationship issues as soon as possible, then proceed to address their exit goals and plans. If necessary, co-owners in this situation should consider outside advisors experienced in mediating and resolving the conflict. If the co-owners are unable to establish a functional relationship with one another, in this author's experience that will lead to one of two outcomes: either one or more co-owners exit under acrimonious conditions, or all the co-owners find themselves trapped together without a foreseeable resolution.

IX

Conclusion—Stepping Forward to Success

A successful exit is the capstone in a business owner's career. It is the opportunity to achieve financial freedom, create the freedom to do what you want and when you want to, and usher forth a sustainable, well-led company that embodies your values and standards.

Despite this, many owners do not cherish preparing for exit. Getting ready for exit takes hard work, on top of regular business needs and demands. Most owners wait too long to get started. Achieving a successful exit requires thinking about and working on exit years in advance of the actual event.

There may be moments during the journey to exit that are not enjoyable. The obstacles are many. Co-owners, employees, customers, family, money, and taxes can all pose a challenge. You may find yourself on uncertain ground without much personal experience to guide you; this may be you (and your co-owners') first and only exit. During difficult times, keep in mind the good you and your co-owners seek to accomplish. You and your co-owners already have accomplished the most important step together— you built a winning business. Now it is time for you and your co-owners to take the remaining steps toward a successful exit.

Exit planning is essentially about identifying and implementing the tactics and tools that enhance business value, and harnessing that value to achieve personal and business goals. Phrased only slightly differently, exit planning is taking a few extra steps while on a long and sometimes challenging journey to assure that the rewards you achieve, the lessons you learn, and the opportunities you create are shared with as many people as possible for as long as possible.

Bibliography

The author recommends the following authors and their books for further reading on the subject of successfully exiting from your business.

1. Covey, Stephen R. *The 7 Habits of Highly Effective People.* Provo, UT: Franklin Covey, 1998.

2. Gerber, Michael E. *The E-Myth Revisited: Why Most Small Businesses Don't Work and What to Do About It.* New York: Harper Collins, 1995.

3. Lencioni, Patrick. *The Advantage: Why Organizational Health Trumps Everything Else in Business.* San Francisco: Jossey-Bass, 2012.

4. Mercer, Z. Christopher. *Buy-Sell Agreements for Baby Boomer Business Owners.* The Baby Boomer Business Owner Transition Guide Series. Peabody Publishing, LP, 2013.

5. Patterson, Kerry. *Crucial Conversations: Tools for Talking When Stakes Are High.* New York: McGraw-Hill, 2002.

6. Scott, Susan. *Fierce Conversations: Achieving Success at Work and in Life One Conversation at a Time.* London: Piatkus, 2003.

7. Ungashick, Patrick. *Dance in the End Zone: The Business Owner's Exit Planning Playbook.* Alpharetta, GA: BookLogix, 2013.

Also By Patrick Ungashick

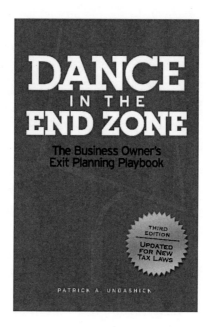

Available at www.patrickungashick.com,
Shop.BookLogix.com, Amazon.com, Apple iBooks, and
BarnesandNoble.com

About the Author

Patrick Ungashick has been helping business owners plan for and create successful exits for more than twenty-five years. He has worked with owners of businesses in a wide variety of industries, from as small as several million in revenues to more than half a billion. Patrick is the author of *Dance in the End Zone: The Business Owner's Exit Planning Playbook* and has been quoted in the *Wall Street Journal*, *New York Times*, *Financial Week*, and other print and radio media. An acclaimed international speaker, he addresses dozens of business groups each year on working toward a successful exit. Patrick has three children and lives with his wife, Maggie, in the Atlanta area.